The Poetics of Religious Experience

The Institute of Ismaili Studies
Occasional Papers—1

The Poetics of Religious Experience

The Islamic Context

AZIZ ESMAIL

I. B. Tauris
LONDON • NEW YORK
in association with
The Institute of Ismaili Studies
LONDON

Published in 1998 by
I.B. Tauris & Co Ltd
Victoria House
Bloomsbury Square
London WC1B 4DZ

175 Fifth Avenue
New York NY 10010

in association with
The Institute of Ismaili Studies
42–44 Grosvenor Gardens
London SW1W 0EB

In the United States of America
and in Canada distributed by
St Martin's Press
175 Fifth Avenue
New York NY 10010

A full CIP record for this book is available from the British Library
A full CIP record for this book is available from the Library of
Congress

ISBN 1 86064 240 3

Library of Congress catalog card number: available

Typeset in ITC New Baskerville by Hepton Books, Oxford
Printed and bound in Great Britain by WBC Ltd, Bridgend

The Institute of Ismaili Studies

The Institute of Ismaili Studies was established in 1977 with the object of promoting scholarship and learning on Islam, in the historical as well as contemporary contexts, and a better understanding of its relationship with other societies and faiths.

The Institute's programmes encourage a perspective which is not confined to the theological and religious heritage of Islam, but seek to explore the relationship of religious ideas to broader dimensions of society and culture. They thus encourage an interdisciplinary approach to the materials of Islamic history and thought. Particular attention is also given to issues of modernity that arise as Muslims seek to relate their heritage to the contemporary situation.

Within the Islamic tradition, the Institute's programmes seek to promote research on those areas which have, to date, received relatively little attention from scholars. These include the intellectual and literary expressions of Shi'ism in general, and Ismailism in particular.

In the context of Islamic societies, the Institute's programmes are informed by the full range and diversity of cultures in which Islam is practised today, from the Middle East, Southern and Central Asia and Africa to the industrialized societies of the West, thus taking into consideration the variety of contexts which shape the ideals, beliefs and practices of the faith.

The publications of the Institute fall into several distinct categories:

1. Occasional papers or essays addressing broad themes of the

relationship between religion and society in the historical as well as modern contexts, with special reference to Islam, but encompassing, where appropriate, other faiths and cultures.
2. Proceedings of conferences or symposia.
3. Works exploring a specific theme or aspect of Islamic faith or culture, or the contribution of an individual figure or writer.
4. Translations of poetic or literary texts.
5. Editions or translations of significant texts of a primary or secondary nature.
6. Ismaili studies.

This publication comes under category one.

In facilitating these and other publications, the Institute's sole aim is to encourage original, interesting and mature thought, scholarship and analysis of the relevant issues. There will naturally be a diversity of views, ideas and interpretations, and the opinions expressed, will be those of the authors.

Preface

The work which follows is essentially an essay in interpretation. It seeks to apply a point of view, which modern philosophers of language have made available to us, to aspects of the Islamic religious tradition. It was conceived, however, in a context which required it to be addressed to a general rather than specialist readership, and to be written, hence, in an expository mode rather than as a research monograph. This explains the didactic and illustrative approach in some parts of the text. Where, especially, a student of modern philosophy and literary criticism may take certain concepts (like those of hermeneutic philosophy) for granted, I have found it necessary to explain, elaborate, and sometimes simplify them. It is hoped, therefore, that a reader already familiar with such concepts will read it with this intended context in mind.

At the same time, it would be idle to deny that the essay aspires to make an original contribution to thinking about Islam (though with what success it is not, of course, for me to judge). The point of view urged here is not one traditionally applied to the subject-matter treated here ('traditional' refers here not only to Islamic normative writing but also to standard scholarship on Islam). Whatever debate the argument advanced in these pages might help to generate, it is hoped that it will be found at least to be worth serious consideration.

Nor is the point of view proposed here important for intellectual reasons alone. It has something to say, even if very tangentially, to wider questions of society and culture. There is a strong case for suggesting that some of the issues dwelt on in this essay—such as the place of the sacred in human culture— are no less important in society than the more obvious and urgent issues of the day, like questions of political governance and economic development. This is certainly true of the industrialised world. But even in developing countries, where appalling problems of poverty, injustice, and war occupy centre-stage, and where debates of a philosophical nature may seem a luxury at best and a wasteful distraction at worst, questions of this sort have, arguably, a definite relation to more urgent and inescapable problems of the day. The relationship may be indirect, and extremely complicated, but it is there. In the Muslim world, this connection may be discerned more easily than in some other societies. It is not hard to see that the way that Islam is conceived in these societies has real consequences on everyday life; and that alternative conceptions of Islamic culture may therefore support, and perhaps even encourage, alternative modes of life in society.

Being an extended argument, the essay has been written as a single piece and is hence intended to be read as a whole. Its various sections do not constitute chapters as such—rather, they mark stages in the progress of the general argument.

All translations from primary sources, except otherwise indicated, are my own.

I would like to thank Alnoor Merchant for his diligent assistance in ensuring consistency of transliteration, format, footnotes, etc., and Kutub Kassam for his meticulous copy-editing and general editorial assistance in getting the text ready for publication.

I would also like to thank my secretary, Rita Bishopp, for transposing my hand-written manuscript, with its numerous, successive emendations and insertions, into the computer.

I

The title of this essay calls for preliminary comment. By 'poetics' I do not only mean poetry, and by 'religious experience' what I have in mind is not those dramatic moments of vision or revelation reported by mystics, but something much more general. It is worth, therefore, dwelling on these concepts a little at the outset. For this will not only throw light on these terms as they are used here, but also help to anticipate the argument of this essay.

At the heart of every religion there is a vision. But a religion is both more and less than the vision which it contains. It is more because, if we think of a vision as a conscious process—a cognitive or imaginative activity—it is clear that members of a religious culture do not lead their daily lives by seeking somehow to re-enact this vision in their minds. The vision, rather, conditions their interpretation of the world and their life with another. Their habits of thought, emotion, and speech, the way they perceive and relate to one another, the judgements of value they habitually make, the ideals to which they give common consent—all these factors show a nucleus of convictions about the world; about what counts as ultimately real and important, worth one's wholehearted commitment and striving. It is this nucleus of principles which I here call a 'vision'. It will be clear, then, that there is no means of access to these core values other than the culture which shapes the life of a given people. The vision is *implicit* in the culture. It is not spelt out in stated principles at first, and then 'translated', as it were, into social rules and cultural practices. It is, from the very first, embodied in a way of life.

Although the nucleus of convictions and values exists nowhere but in a society's totality of forms—its institutions, traditions, codes

1

of doctrine, and rules of behaviour—the symbolic core or nucleus transcends these forms. The forms represent an *interpretation* of the visionary core. It is important to note the wider (or perhaps deeper) sense in which the term 'interpretation' is meant here, as opposed to what it is taken to mean in common parlance. We tend to associate the word with a conscious, cognitive activity, as is shown by the fact that we think of it as something carried out by judges (who strive to interpret a nation's constitution) or by theologians (who construct intellectual systems of belief by interpreting scripture). But cultural practices may as readily be seen as interpretations. Only, in this case, the interpretative activity is *de facto*: implicit or unconscious. If we compare child-rearing practices, for instance, in Japan or rural India on the one hand and a Western society on the other, we are bound to notice deep-lying differences. In the one case, the child is likely to be expected to be modest or retiring in the presence of adults: contrary behaviour will be condemned as too 'forward'; whereas in the other case, such hesitancy will be a source of worry to the parents. The child will be thought to lack social confidence, or to suffer from inner anxieties which make it 'withdrawn' or 'introverted'; and a counsellor will duly be called in to help. Such counselling, if proffered in the opposite social context, would be condemned as inciting insolence, aggression, or vanity. Child-rearing practices are, in this sense, interpretations on the part of a culture, of what it means to be human, and how one ought to live. By studying such practices in a particular culture, as an anthropologist might do, one would be able to infer the world-view of the people in question. In effect, the anthropologist interprets the interpretation of life which a given culture, or a given set of social practices, represents. Through the facts of that culture, one can discern, sometimes clearly, at other times hazily, the vision of life which lies behind and underneath that culture, shaping and inspiring it from within.

There is yet another element implied in the idea of interpretation, and this too deserves to be noted. When we speak of something as an interpretation, our attention is tacitly drawn not only to what is, but to what is not. To put it another way: we notice a bounded space, even as we become aware, by the same token, of a space beyond. For, to say that something is an interpretation is to imply that it is but one form of actualisation. In its very specificity, it suggests the possibility of alternatives—of unrealised possibilities, options other than the one at hand. When an anthropologist describes the interpretation of the world in the culture observed by him, in the background of this description there is an awareness that there are other ways, as the saying goes, of slicing the cake—other strategies of ordering and making sense of the world. The anthropologist's work is permeated by this awareness because he is an outsider, at least in a part of his mind, to the group that he studies. This fact, and the nature of the anthropologist's training, which aims at a thorough appreciation of the relativity of cultures, is what makes him conscious of the contingent character of what he studies.

The historian is similarly conscious of the contingent quality of the events and phenomena he or she studies, a contingency operating, in his case, not in place but in time. While attending to what happened, a historian with the necessary gift of imagination is simultaneously conscious of what might have happened, but failed to do so. After all, the events of human history are circumstantial. Had other decisions been taken or other personalities been present at a significant time or place, had nature intervened through an earlier death or the prolongation of a life, or had, indeed, the weather been different on a fateful day—the course of events that the historian narrates might, as he well knows, have been significantly different. These academic examples point to a wider, human experience—the experience, namely, of life as both closed and open; of facts which cannot be undone and possibilities not yet done with; of meanings which have taken shape, and meaning which is yet to be shaped. We are creatures of constraint; but creatures, nonetheless, with a sense of the infinite. Insofar as we have this sense, we are free—not free enough to experience or attain everything, but free by virtue of being able to imagine the infinite, and therefore, to this extent, capable of transcending, through forward imagination and effort, the finiteness of the given, the present.

These considerations take us very close to the heart of religious vision. For the concept of God, so pivotal in the religious imaginations of the Judaic, Christian, and Islamic traditions, represents both the outermost limit of human conception, as well as the source of ideals which speak of the fulfillment of human nature. The infinite distance of the divine from the human goes hand in hand with its infinite proximity to the human. Like the horizon it is ever so near and ever so far. This interplay of the 'here' and the 'there', of the finite and the infinite, is also an interplay of the given and the ideal, of what is and what can yet be. It is the essence of prophecy: you are such and such, but yet maybe otherwise. 'This' world—the given world—and the 'other' world—the ideal world, the world of the hereafter—are metaphorical variants on this vast and common theme.

This, however, is to run ahead of our present discussion. Let us return to the theme of interpretation. We have seen that to consider a given piece of activity or tradition as an interpretation is to note its contingent character. This is a reflection of life itself, which has two aspects: finiteness, manifest in limitations of physical nature, the irreversibility of time, and the certainty of death; and on the other hand, an openness inherent in experiences of hope, faith, and striving after an ideal. There is, however, a special situation in which interpretation occurs, a situation which is of great importance in the life of a culture. This is the continual activity of interpreting which takes place within a tradition. An important question one may ask about this activity is: what premises, what implicit assumptions, underlie the practice of continual reinterpretation within a tradition?

There is a central, if tacit, premise in all such activity. This is the premise that the nucleus of values which give character and identity to a tradition is not exhausted by the intellectual, moral, and practical system in which it may be embodied at a given time. This sense is especially strong at moments when the circumstances of a community are in the process of being transformed, due to shifts either in internal complexion or in the socio-political environment. In such conditions, the stewardship of a tradition may consist in relying on this intuition, so as to reap the harvest of new fruit from old seeds; and thus to draw new insights from the originating ideals of the civilisation in question.

This search is usually accompanied by the assumption of a distinction between the essential and the ephemeral. It is not fruitful to take this distinction too literally: to draw up a list of fundamental principles and distinguish them from other secondary doctrines. It is more helpful to take a further step and inquire into the intuitions *behind* distinctions of this sort in the first place. One of the important intuitions here is the *open texture* of the core values at the heart of a historical civilisation. Unless this premise is taken seriously, the reference of the present to the past, or the past to the present, has no logical force. For, if a historical tradition is to be regarded as a process rather than a monument—a river rather than a quarry, ever-flowing rather than a fixed storehouse of fixed products—the relationship between continuity and change has to be seen as similarly complex. No culture ever begins at an absolute starting point, at a Cartesian spot, suitably cleared of all presuppositions. On the other hand, no living tradition can honestly sustain itself by reference to a static standard or model derived from the past. A living tradition proceeds on the basis of a continual re-making, not only of the new in terms of the old, but also of the old in terms of the new. New dimensions are continually added to old ideas under the impetus of new experience; just as old themes are found to resonate in what may at first sight seem wholly novel. This is what lends force to the observation of one of the most acute literary minds of this century, T. S. Eliot, that 'traditions ... cannot be inherited'; they are something acquired only 'by great labour'.

In a religious tradition, this 'labour' consists of testing new conceptions against its symbolic nucleus, and testing the latter against the former. But in speaking of the 'symbolic nucleus', I mean to emphasise another element in this picture. It is advisedly that I speak of the core ideas of a religious vision as symbols, instead of equating them with what are often called 'fundamental principles'. The difference may not be immediately obvious; if obvious, it may still not be, at first glance, persuasive. After all, we habitually think of religion as a system of beliefs; and we are as

often inclined to divide the beliefs of a particular religion into
those that are fundamental to it, that is without which it would
cease to be itself, and those which are not essential for it to be
what it is. But it is worth bearing in mind that the description of
religion in terms of beliefs is a latter-day, not an original, event in
its history. It is also dependent upon a specific enterprise, namely
that of codification. The history of Islam illustrates this very well.
The Qur'an does not urge its listeners to subscribe to propositions of belief. What it does is to summon them to an outlook on
life, and to action commensurate with that outlook. Philosophy
and deed, ethic and act, are fused together, so that each imparts
meaning to the other. It is this which forms the substance of the
Qur'an, whereas the codification of principles (*usul*) in terms of
belief in God, prophecy, scripture, etc., however justifiable by reference to the Qur'an, is a later historical development.

This difference becomes clear if we consider the circumstances
surrounding the revelation of the Qur'an on the one hand, and
the emergence of doctrine, or articles of belief, on the other. One
of the things which is meant in describing the Qur'an as revelation is that it was a charismatic event. The Prophet Muhammad
preached out of a sense of personal calling. It should not be forgotten that the Qur'an denotes the *event* of recitation. Only
subsequently did it become, in physical terms, a book. The recitation was felt and received as inspired, and inspiration suggests
openness. It is not something directed to preconceived goals or
conclusions. The revelation as an event, a process, showed history
in the making, not the unfolding of a static body of truths. It is
this openness, and presence of a vision and an ethic, as opposed
to theological or legal systems, which is crucial to the character of
the Qur'an as an 'event'. The systems emerged, no doubt out of
genuine historical need, over the course of time. Thus, for example, the reference to God in the Qur'an is of a very different sort
from that in debates characteristic of theology, about what kind
of being God is. Similarly, the ethical content of the Qur'an may
be distinguished from its positive injunctions in matters such as
inheritance, punishment, and commerce.

The codification of faith in terms of articles of belief and practice, and the codification of ethics into statutes, was a product of jurisprudence. Islamic jurisprudence was the product of a very different era from that of the Qur'an, and of a very different society. It was a society more sophisticated, urban, and imperial, above all more diversified, than that in which the revelation had taken place. In this new atmosphere, Islam, which was for a long time the faith of a minority, reigning over a vast and far-flung empire, with old institutions and ancient, sophisticated cultures, had to be reconstituted as a basis of the new order. In this process, several rich currents of thought and practice—Greek methods in logic and philosophy, Judaic and Christian traditions, ancient Iranian literature and Roman jurisprudence—inevitably informed Islamic thought; though this is to say something very different from the claim that bad Orientalism used to make, namely that Islamic thought was a 'borrowed' rather than original creation. The short retort to this claim has to be that no originality ever occurs in a vacuum; and that originality does not mean the descent from heaven, as it were, of ideas or institutions never encountered before. It lies, rather, in a process of creativity, whereby something genuinely new is born out of a previous environment. Of such creativity classical Islam is a superb example. But it is also a fact that classical Islam is not the same thing as the Qur'anic vision, though it is not disconnected from it; just as modern Islam, even when it sees itself as a pure revival of classical Islam, is in fact a very different phenomenon. In general, even the exact restatement of a past adage turns out, in altered circumstances, to be a new statement. For the same phrase in two different contexts will have a different meaning and significance; and will therefore be, to all intents and purposes, anything but 'same'.

I should perhaps add, to forestall a possible misunderstanding, that I do not mean to set up a simple contrast between the Qur'an and the succeeding history of Islam—a contrast that many modern Muslim writers, committed to reform of one kind or another, tend to emphasise. I do not suggest that latter-day Islam was a deviation from the Qur'anic model, because in an objective understanding there is no place for concepts like 'deviation'. Nor do I say that classical Islam is historically conditioned while the Qur'an is not. The fact that the Qur'an has spoken and continues to speak, poignantly and powerfully, to innumerable followers through the course of centuries shows that something in it is time-less. But this 'something' needs to be distinguished from such phenomena as ordinances of war and truce, reactions to local 'others', whether Jews, Christians, or the Meccan Quraysh, codes of punishment, etc., all of which were clearly conditioned by local and regional circumstances. Rather than distinguishing between fundamental beliefs and not-so-fundamental applications—a procedure which is as mechanical as it is methodologically dubious—it is ultimately more fruitful to inquire into what this problem might reveal about the nature of faith. And one good answer to this question is in terms of a distinction between symbolic conceptions and doctrinal concepts.

The distinguishing feature of symbolic conceptions is that they are what we might call leading notions: open, elastic, and indeterminate. A good illustration of a symbolic conception is the notion of a final judgement, which is so germane to the Judaic, Christian, and Islamic traditions. As a symbol, it represents an ideal of justice and an ideal resolution of life, where virtuous action and well-being coincide. Such an outcome is seldom realised in actual experience. But as what we might call a 'horizon idea', it provides a foundation for moral life. Similarly, the notion of the Last Day declares that change, decay, and death are not the last word on the question of the meaning of life. The more general and embryonic this notion remains, the more fertile it will prove in suggesting diverse interpretations. The more theologically definite it becomes, the narrower will be the range of ideas it is capable of suggesting. Narratives of what is supposed to happen beyond death are purely speculative, having little impact in the here and now. But there is an alternative way of looking at them, i.e., as symbolisations of a dimension of existence in the here and now. On this, Wittgenstein's remarks are thought-provoking:

> Death is not an event in life: we do not live to experience death. If we take eternity to mean not infinite temporal duration but timeless-ness, then eternal life belongs to those who live in the present.[1]

The quest for the meaning of life, given its finiteness, can lead to many different attempts, not necessarily exclusive, to transcend its brevity: in pious hope for life after death, however conceived; in mystical realisation of a spiritual dimension, transcending the mundane, in the here and now; and not least, through the commitment of one's life to a better and more equitable future for all. The symbols of 'another' life are open-ended symbols, with a plethora of associations, with the potential to grow and develop in new directions, and assimilate new nuances of meaning.

We are now in a position to sum up some of the propositions contained in the title of this essay. We saw that 'religious experience' is meant here in the widest rather than the narrowest sense. It refers to a vision of being, present in core-symbols, which provides an orientation to life and guides ethical conduct in the world. We saw that this vision is both more and less than the entirety of a religion: less because religion is always an embodiment (which is to say, an interpretation, in the sense indicated above). It is also more, because the core-symbols are not exhausted by the forms which may prevail in a given time or place. On the contrary, they are capable of supporting new and unforeseen nuances of meaning in ongoing history. Lastly, the symbolic character of these conceptions is what gives rise to poetics. This concept also needs preliminary exploration before the introductory section can be brought to a close.

By 'poetics' what is meant here is something more then poetry, though poetry is part of it. It refers to creativity of a particular kind, namely exploration in language. The kind of language which lends itself to exploration is the language of symbol and metaphor. The nature of this language will become clearer if we contrast it to a kind of language which gives information.

Unlike the language of information, poetic language does not state facts. The statement, on a given occasion, that it is dark outside (say, owing to a power failure, or to a lack of street lighting) is a plain, literal assertion of fact. Its truth or falseness can be checked by observation by anyone who has normal eyesight and knows the meaning of the word 'dark'. However, when in *Macbeth*, Shakespeare makes Banquo say to his son as they grope their way in the thick of the night, shortly after we have been let into Macbeth and his wife's wicked scheme to murder the King of Scotland, so that (in line with the witches' prophecy) Macbeth may gain the throne—when, against this background, Shakespeare makes Banquo exclaim: 'There's husbandry in heaven, their candles are all out ...,' we know at once, in our deepest being, that something considerably more is said in these lines than that the night is dark. The difference is not simply between plain and ornamental speech. It is a question of the *scope* of meaning. What Banquo sees in the darkened sky is not solely a reflection of his own fears and concerns. It is a suspicion, a foreboding vision, of something looming there, encompassing the universe, in the shape of an objective menace. Of this, the personal careers of various protagonists are a partial reflection. Thus, the text unfolds on several levels at once. It depicts the lives and characters of its protagonists. But in doing so, it also makes statements about the kind of world in which such men and women live; in which mysterious forces, beyond their intellectual control, play on them.

Thus, while being all too concrete, the words quoted here have the force of an impersonal, universal statement. They do not only remind us that a heinous murder is about to occur. They tell us something much more, something which is true on a cosmic scale. This cosmic statement may be put simply as follows: there is Evil abroad. Since what is evoked here is the scheme of things entire, and not merely a single incident in space or time, it is not just an evil episode with which we are brought face to face, but Evil as a cosmic principle. Here another very important point deserves to be noted. On this level, which we may call the metaphysical level, there is no statement which is not at the same time a question. This is shown, above all, in what such language *does* to a listener or reader. Statements inform us; questions challenge us. When we hear 'Evil is abroad,' we are moved, perplexed, and stirred into an interrogation of being. Out of the bewilderment which comes no sooner than the terror of this recognition dawns on us, we think of our own lives, our own experience. We wonder whether we have not ourselves encountered, or observed in others, the power of an incomprehensible destiny in human life. We ask ourselves what this could mean. We search for ways in which to fathom this experience, to see it in some kind of perspective, and if possible, to go beyond it. We are reminded of the opposite principle of Evil, the principle of Good, celebrated both in classical philosophy and in religious scripture. Jews and Christians may be reminded of the Book of Job. Christians may remember the Passion of Christ. And Muslims may well recall the all-too-vivid evocation of an evil which shuts out all light, blots out all vision, in the following passage of the Qur'an:

> Like the darkness in a fathomless sea darkened
> by wave above wave,
> and above it all, clouds.
> Layers over layers of dark.
> If one stretches forth his hand he can scarcely see it.
> For he for whom God has not set up a light, has no light.[2]

What we find in poetry like Shakespeare's are echoes of symbols which were first given in the Judaeo–Christian, Islamic, and Classical traditions. Poetic traditions in the cultures derived from these sources have been continually nourished and replenished by these original symbols. It was in the Biblical, Qur'anic, and in a few other sites in the world, that long-enduring fundamental intimations about the human experience of being were revealed. To be sure, religious vision cannot be reduced to poetry; it is much more than that. Religious meaning binds a whole community, an entire society, through a narrative of beginnings and ends, i.e., of human existence interpreted in the frame of cosmic time and space. The point of such narrative is to give meaning to human life, but also, in so doing, to induce meaningful action, i.e., action oriented to ethical ends. Poetry is only a specialised pursuit within this civilisational totality. But the language of poetry, especially poetry which seeks to speak of being as a whole, is a good example of a kind of language which differs from straightforward propositions of fact. It shows a way of thinking and speaking in which metaphor, symbol, and analogy are of the essence; which challenges the imagination, feeling, and reason, and thus engenders creativity.

In short, such language is semantically pregnant. It has a way of radiating outwards—laterally, above, and into the depths. This element of continual inquiry is also what we find, in a different form, in science. Observation stimulates further inquiry in science, and knowledge builds on knowledge. For, the scientist is a poet of nature; just as the poet is a scientist of the heart. Nothing is further from the argument of this essay than the false opposition, encountered so often in modern times, of the poetic or humanistic to the scientific mind; of intuition to intellect; or of science to religion. These dichotomies, to which I shall return, are products of modern European history. The contrast with which I am concerned here lies elsewhere. It is a contrast between two models of knowledge, one of which sees acquisition of facts as its essence, while the other is an exploratory model. Statements of fact tend to fill and satiate; whereas poetic, philosophical, or scientific thought, while no doubt dealing with facts, whets renewed hunger. Furthermore, it is critical in spirit. And there is something of this spirit—we may call it, in a sense to be explained later, the prophetic spirit—at the heart of religious experience.

The language of faith enunciates the bond between man and what he perceives or experiences as sacred. The sacred cannot be captured in propositions of fact. There is something about it which makes symbolic expression especially suited to it. Several points need to be noted in this connection. First, the sacred is always perceived in the context of a *relationship*. It is never grasped as an object in itself. While God is depicted in the Qur'an, for instance, as the Absolute, having attributes radically free of the limitations of creatureliness, significantly the revelation of God occurs there primarily in a dialogical context. God *speaks*, and this speech is the most consequential act as far as human affairs are concerned. For the divine is not contemplated as if by a spectator. Hence the limitations of theology, which is an intellectual contemplation of God. The divine is primordially revealed in a dialogical act. In the Qur'an, humanity is addressed either directly or indirectly through the figure of a messenger or prophet. Reciprocally, the prophet, or the humanity which he represents, enters into a verbal exchange (through prayer, etc.) with the divine.

The second principle follows from the first. The importance of the relational aspect means that the sacred becomes known to man in forms which reflect human psychology and culture. In one form or another, the human relation with the divine involves intermediation. I shall return to this point later. Thirdly, the relationship of man to his own being, and to the being of all things, is by its very nature manifold rather than singular. This implies, as its logical corollary, the legitimacy of spiritual pluralism. Lastly, the indeterminacy of language about the sacred, which was noted above as a characteristic of symbolic language, argues not only against literalism, but in favour of a continuing rather than completed symbolisation.

The rest of the essay is devoted to elaborating the themes broached throughout this introductory section. As these themes are addressed in the Islamic context, I shall illustrate them mostly with Islamic examples; though they are, in fact, of more general importance, applicable to the study of other religious traditions, and indeed, to wider issues of culture.[3]

II

The epic poem of Jalal al-Din Rumi, the Iranian mystic, opens with these famous lines:

> Listen to the reed,
> how it tells a tale
> complaining of separation:
> Ever since I was parted
> from the reed-bed,
> my lament has made
> men and women weep.
> I search for a heart
> smitten by separation
> that I may tell the pain
> of love-desire.
> Everyone who has got far from his source
> harks back for the time
> when he was one with it.[4]

The first important thing in reading these lines is to forget what they state and try to listen to what they say. What I mean is the following. These lines are famous among scholars and followers of mysticism. Students of mysticism are learned in mystical *doctrine*—in *systems* of mystical *thought*. Armed with the doctrine, they find in these lines an eloquent restatement, a confirmation of what they already believe in: that the human soul is separated from God; that it yearns to be reunited with Him; that this yearning and the pain of separation are a closed book to someone who has not had these feelings; and that the path to reunion is through love. But this is already a system of beliefs. 'Soul' and 'God' are concepts with a long and varied theological history. The concepts of 'source' and 'separation' may seem straightforward and self-evident. Their very clarity, however, is a trap. For we do not find it mysterious when someone says that the source of the Nile is in Lake Victoria. We may find it absurd if someone said that the Nile was longing to return to Lake Victoria; but we are unlikely to find it mysterious. We may conclude that the speaker was trying to make a not too successful joke; or that he was being perverse; or that his imagination was dubiously overactive. Whatever we may think, it will not strike us, other things being equal, that the remark conceals a mystery to be explored. What, though, when it is said that life itself—not this or that object, nor this or that item of living experience, but life itself—is headed a certain way? From what vantage point can we map the direction of life, or of the world, when we do not stand outside it but are part of it? A way of speaking which at first sight resembles ordinary ways of speaking turns out, on reflection, to be mysterious. The poetry works on us: it strikes a chord, evokes something within us. Yet we cannot paraphrase it into a statement. We cannot honestly say, when we ponder on these words, that speaking about one's 'source' and 'destiny' is clear in the ordinary sense of the word 'clear'. But we cannot say that it is absurd either—not, at any rate, unless we are prepared to dismiss whole traditions of discourse as absurd. What the poetry evokes is a mystery. And without being in too much of a hurry to solve the mystery, and without, on the other hand, simply assuming it as a 'mystery', it is more rewarding to inquire:

what manner of speaking is this? What does it say about human language (and hence about human life)?

Lastly, the concept of love. Textbooks on mysticism tell us, over and over again, that the mystic path (in the Islamic case, the Sufi path) is that of love. But what does this mean? In ordinary speech, we use the word 'love' in many different ways. We do not speak of 'love of knowledge' in the same sense as we speak of 'making love'; and these examples can be multiplied. All such usages of 'love' have what a modern philosopher has called 'family resemblance': it is not purely arbitrary, a freak of our speech, that we use the same word in all these different contexts, and only in these contexts. Nevertheless they differ, and the differences are especially great when we compare different historical periods or cultures. The phenomenon of 'courtly love' in medieval Europe, where one admired a lady from a distance and pined for her, gladly submitting to every ordeal on the way, was a chivalrous convention specific to social forms of the time and place. That convention died with the disappearance of the feudal order. Romantic love, for a long time a subject for singers, poets, dreamers, artists, madmen, and those feigning madness (in the Islamic cultural context, the story of Layla and Majnun readily comes to mind), received a considerable blow with the growth of new patterns of sexual behaviour due to changes in life brought about by modern industrial society. It is unnecessary to labour this point further. The morale is that what we take for granted as a universal human emotion reflects not one but many experiences. These experiences are conditioned by social facts and historical traditions. And even apart from all this, the language employed can often pose a riddle. Such, eminently, is the case with the phrase, 'love of God'. For what can this mean, when, to start with, the concept of God is anything but straightforward; when it does not represent a simple act of naming, but engages, instead, the whole intellect and imagination?

Religious traditions harbour intimations about the sacred foundations of life. But religious traditions tend in a twofold direction: they reveal, and they conceal. As mentioned above, the basic function of religious preaching is to elaborate a symbolic universe. Over time, the symbols are absorbed into superstructures of doctrine. Doctrines are propositions which demand belief. The intellectual justification of religious belief is what is known as theology. These intellectual formations are among the most impressive creations of the human mind. Structures of belief and doctrine are a source of religious identity; they enable people to belong to traditions, to societies organised under common symbols of authority. They determine the shape of human thoughts and feelings. And because they are shared, they constitute a common culture. They are a source of moral norms associated with a way of life. And they serve as charters—legitimations of ritual acts which demonstrate the relation of man to the sacred.

But systems of belief and doctrine are secondary or tertiary phenomena. They come after, whether in time or in their inner logic, to the primary symbols which express the belonging of man to the sacred. The primary symbols transcend the division of world cultures, or the division within cultures, into what we call the 're- ligious' and the 'secular'. From time to time, therefore, it is useful to free the mind of these kinds of categories, and to listen afresh to the language in which the basic dilemmas and enigmas of life have been traditionally articulated.

Let us reflect for a moment on Rumi's opening lines without the mental intervention of qualifiers like 'mystical' or 'religious', and without immediate reference to the specific doctrines associated with these adjectives. To begin with, let us note that the passage is poetic (in that it is versified). But it is also about poetry, or more generally, about language. Verbal language is only one form of it. The passage itself refers to the music—the organised sound—emitted by the flute. Let us call this 'language' for the time being, so long as we understand the word in its most general rather than verbally specific sense.

The flute utters a sound; but it is more than a sound. It 'tells a tale', a story. The story speaks of an alienation, a lost unity. But language itself is an alienation, for the eloquence of the flute is heard only after its substance has been torn from its 'source'. In the reed-bed, all is silence. The separation precipitates lament; lament is a voice, where previously there was none. It is as though language were born in anguish, the anguish of a rupture. It is a sundering of being of which it speaks; and the paradox is that it is this sundering which is also the source of speech.

But the rupture is not the essence. It is our state, but insofar as our state is one of incompletion, a fragmentation, we are also led to think of a wholeness, a completeness. For rupture presupposes unity; mutilation implies a prior wholeness. Neither concept is imaginable without the other. The *idea* of wholeness arises only when wholeness is missing. Thus, in the same breath (literally *breath*, while speaking of the flute) that the anguish of severance is first voiced, we also hear undertones of a reassuring destiny—a healing of the breach. On one hand, there is a lost paradise. But thanks to the poetic imagination, there is also a faith, a hope which, looking into the distance, sees paradise regained.

It will be obvious that we are far as yet from the language of theology. What has just been said about the incompleteness of being and the accompanying vision of wholeness, is very general. It can be made more specific by transposing it into more definite vocabularies. One such vocabulary is that of mysticism. For this is precisely what the mystics mean when they say that man is other than God, but that 'essentially' he is one with God. Even this, however, is not yet theology. It is symbolic language which will grow into theology only with the aid of Greek metaphysical concepts like 'essence' and 'attributes'. It was the task of theology to codify symbols into secondary doctrine. Sufi doctrine is but one example of this, and when we encounter this doctrine in secondary works, where it is set out as a system of beliefs or principles, we are already several steps away from the primary symbols which are human *before* they are culturally specific, and poetic before they are specifically religious. Thus, what we now have in front of us are manicured gardens which bear only indirect witness to the original exuberance of nature.

Let us, therefore, stay at the 'concept-free' level of the poetry we have been considering. At this level, what the poetry says (through its symbols) speaks about the human condition at large. The metaphors of separation or estrangement ring true at many levels of human experience. Let us take language itself. At first sight, it would seem that language and estrangement have nothing to do with each other; only a forced interpretation could bring these otherwise heterogeneous ideas together. But on closer consideration it will be apparent that language involves both contact and separation. By the simple act of naming things or objects, we 'grasp' them. By its act of naming, and the classification of experience, more generally through parts of speech, language generates an order. Through this order, the world becomes accessible to thought and action. But when objects are named, they also withdraw, as it were, into a distance. They disengage themselves from one's being. They stand apart. They take on boundaries, and especially consequential among these is the line which demarcates self from world. Objects stand 'out there' in relation to the spectator-self. The division of the world into subject and object is intrinsic to the very act of naming.

An example of this ambivalence is to be found in science. Science gives us knowledge about the world. It brings the world under human mastery. Interestingly, science becomes possible only when the human contact with the world is disciplined into a controlled, curtailed engagement. It is a precondition of progress in science that our ordinary, affective relationship to the world be suspended. No doubt, science is nourished by imagination: it is imagination which suggests questions, hypotheses, and connections between otherwise discrete phenomena. But science also demands that the imagination must not run away with itself; that it must avoid what we call flights of fancy. This partial disengagement of the personality from the world is what gives it power, paradoxically, over the world: the power to annex the world to the empire of knowledge. We pay tribute to the power of disengagement through the ideal of what we aptly call 'objectivity'.

But the glory of science comes casting a shadow in its trail. A certain disquiet has accompanied the forward march of science through human history. This discontent has found expression in different terms during different periods. There was the sense, in the romantic phase of modern history, that science had stripped the world of magic, and that art was needed to give some of the magic back to nature. (This theory is open to question, for a sense of wonder and mystery is quite central to science.) Again from the middle of this century onwards, when nuclear fission was seen as a measure of the infinite possibilities of science, there was widespread fear that human knowledge and human wisdom might expand in inverse proportions to each other. Today the same fear stalks the growing field of biotechnology. The social sciences, on their part, have to contend with the charge that the application of scientific objectivity to human affairs can at best yield limited success. It is said, in this connection, that there are limits to the kind of objectivity essential to the natural sciences when this is extended to the study of man. The issue of language is all-important in the social sciences. It includes the question of the language of social science itself.

Implied in all this is something more fundamental, which has to do with the ethics of knowledge. The relevant issue here is that of the relation of knowledge to being—the power of knowledge to unite as well as estrange. This is a larger issue than that of methods and disciplines of learning. We can hear its germinal echoes in the symbolic narratives in the Judaic, Christian, and Islamic traditions. Adam, says the Qur'an, was taught the names of all things. But Adam is no longer in Paradise; he is exiled.

The story of Adam and Eve is the story of humankind. Adam is Everyman.[5] His fate (and that of Eve) speak of the human condition as a whole. The story has the character of myth. Myths are both true and false: false if taken literally, true as allegories of existence. When we are told that Adam and Eve were 'once upon a time' in the garden, that certain events then took place, and that both were then expelled from their first abode, this time-frame—the linear sequence of events, where one incident follows another—may be read as an event of human experience in the here and now. Time itself is an allegory of 'space', so that the relation of what went 'before' and what came 'after' evokes a relation between surface and depth, nature and culture, matter and spirit. The story suggests that somewhere in one's 'depths' a human being is (speaking metaphorically) one with God; while at another level he is estranged. Similarly, at one level man is in harmony with nature, while at another level, culture and the institutions of society, the laws which make collective existence possible, interpose a distance between our 'natural' and our 'socialised' identities. The messianic dream—the dream of a *qiyama*, when the restrictions of law and social convention will finally be cast aside—has to be interpreted in this context. It is a symbolic aspiration, a longing for 'essential' or 'original' innocence, for 'final' perfection. It is not something which is, or can be, historically enacted. It belongs to that 'other' world of sacred imagination, not 'this' world of social and political organisation. In the ease with which this line between utopian imagination and historical existence may be crossed, messianic movements are face to face with the most seductive peril with which they have to reckon.

The dualism suggested in Rumi's story may also be seen in human relationships. Human beings seek to unite through conversation, friendship, and the intimacy of love. But the desired union is hardly ever complete or enduring. Communication between people is very often hampered by the limitations of language and of mutual comprehension. Failure of communication, and the resulting frustration, is at least as common as success. Friendships form and break. A friend is seldom the Friend—his empathy in some areas of one's life is not always equalled by that in others. In love, there is communion, but only more or less. The act of sexual union epitomises this ambiguity at the heart of existence. The act of love seeks, through the interpenetration of two beings, to overcome separateness. But this is seldom achieved in its entirety; and where it is achieved, it is ephemeral. Moments of union are followed sooner or later by a realisation of separateness. The reverie of night gives way to the dissipated consciousness of day. In all this, the empirical and the ideal coexist without ever coalescing. Such coalescence is what is promised on the Last Day. In life, there is both experience and longing; an awareness of limits, and the spiritually limitless.

There is a sense in which all these are present in Rumi's passage. But what can 'in' mean here? One cannot say they are present in Rumi's mind. One can only say they are present in the language. And this statement too needs to be refined.

The ideas arising from our reading of the passage from Rumi are present in it only in the sense that they are evoked or suggested by it. They are present, in other words, in its symbolic texture. Symbols such as division and separation, the language of lament, union, and integration, are highly resonant. They suggest rather than state, evoke rather than formulate. As symbols, they say a great deal because they do not say any one thing in too narrow or definite a form. Like depth in a painting, they hold meaning in reserve. They generate lines of meaning which emerge and radiate inwards and outwards during the act of reading. They release associations and reverberations. Symbolic language points to a hinterland of meaning. It points to the realm of unconscious meanings, like those which psychoanalysis investigates. It is meaning in a state of *latency*. This is what makes it possible for the great classics of antiquity (including religious scriptures) to have continuing relevance in social and historical contexts far removed from the original. Such re-interpretations are sometimes attacked as arbitrary. At one level, they are indeed arbitrary: to a rational mind, the claim that ancient texts could anticipate events and ideas belonging to a future world can only sound absurd. But in another sense these readings are not arbitrary. For insights into the basic symbolic intimations are indefinite or open enough—embryonic enough—to offer seeds for germination in distant soils and climates.

This difference between what is said in a latent condition of language, and what is stated in explicit or definite terms, may be made more clear by, as it were, magnifying this difference. Instead of comparing levels within verbal language, let us compare language with non-verbal meaning. Music, performance, and ritual come to mind. Let us take dance as our first example. Indian classical dance goes hand in hand with a philosophy which says what this or that gesture 'means'. Similarly, interpretations of ballet frequently paraphrase movements into statements of meaning or emotion. To some extent, such linguistic 'translations' of a physical art strike us as superfluous. Yet they are not altogether misguided. They do illuminate, and in such instances we usually feel they are to the point. But what makes them 'to the point'?

We speak of something nearer our present subject if we ask this question of ritual. Ritual too is an expression. But what kind of expression is it? And what does it express? It may be said, for instance, that the sky is an appropriate symbol of heaven, hence a common tendency towards an upward glance in prayer. By the same token, water may be said to symbolise purity, hence the rites common to many religious traditions of ablution, baptism, sprinkling, or drinking of water. But it is not the case that one first forms the intellectual concept of infinite power and then decides on the sky as its appropriate symbol. Nor do cultures first form the abstract concept of 'purity', and decide, next, on water as the most suitable object to serve as a 'symbol of' this concept. It is rather that height itself suggests, through an inherent sublimation of the physical, the idea of infinite power. And the cleansing properties of water itself suggests, through an inherent sublimation—through metaphorisation—a purity over and above the physical. It is not that the physical is tagged onto the idea like an adhesive label. The fact is rather that human beings experience the world both materially and spiritually. The world is already impregnated with meaning. Matter and spirit are ultimately inseparable, and they are never so firmly united as in the symbol. This is why attempts to render the symbolism of ritual into abstract concepts are ultimately none too satisfactory. To try to substitute a symbolised meaning for a symbol is a project doomed to failure. The symbol *is* its meaning. It and its meaning are inseparable. How is one to tell, as W. B. Yeats was to say, the dancer from the dance?

In the last analysis, ritual resists translation into the conceptual intellect. The demand for intellectualisation—for its 'meaning'—is not a universal occurrence. It arises in historical contexts where the performers' spontaneous participation in the rites has been put into question. As a result of social and cultural change, what might up to now have been assumed (or performed) as part of an ongoing tradition, may now 'stand out', and call for rational justification. It is then that the demand for 'meaning' becomes pressing. But meaning as concept is extraneous to meaning as symbol. The language of philosophy or theology cannot replace the language of poetry. Verbal articulation has no way of replacing, or fully paraphrasing, the physical symbolism of ritual.

This point may be extended to differences within verbal language. The lesson we may draw from the analysis of the *Mathnawi*'s opening passage above is that mystical symbolism is of wider interest than mystical doctrine. For the symbol resonates across a wide range of human experience. Mysticism gives it a particular gloss and interpretation. But the symbols are primordial in relation to doctrine. They transcend the specialised religious consciousness which is characteristic of mysticism. The basic theme in mysticism is a dialectic between separation and union. The self is experienced as fragmentary, and being as divided. This fragmentariness and division are seen as phenomenal rather than real. This theme is characteristically mystical, and its interpretation in terms of separation and union with God makes it religiously mystical. But depth-analysis will show that this symbolism can speak to many minds, and accommodate itself to a variety of beliefs. It has resonance with many areas of human experience. What is identified as a distinctive ideology or 'ism'—'mysticism' or 'Sufism'—is but a particular cultural expression of universal, existential themes.

This thesis of the precedence of existential meaning finds support in an interesting feature of mystical literature. When it is read without preconceptions, mystical literature often gives the impression of a fundamental ambiguity of meaning. This is especially true with regard to its erotic content. It is a commonplace that mystical poetry is often intensely sensual. This is usually explained by its exegetes and commentators—apologists, in fact—as a symbolic device. Because spiritual love, it is said, is impossible to put into words, the categories of human love are the best available means in which to depict the higher relationship. But this explanation is open to several objections. To begin with, there is no experience, other than a simple sensation, which is not mediated through language. Only elementary sensations like pain, heat, or cold, the perception of colours, etc., seem to involve only biological rather than cultural categories. Any experience more complex than sensation is, from the very first, culturally mediated. Moreover, symbolism cannot be reduced to a verbal artifice.

It is not a code-language, designed to state, in disguise, what might be imprudent or otherwise inconvenient to say directly.

Such code-language has its uses: its employment in wartime is a classic example. It is also a feature of speech or writing in societies with strong traditions of censorship. There were circumstances in Islamic societies where (like anywhere else) coded expression was politically expedient. But this has nothing to do with symbolism in the generic sense. This is an irreducible form of expression, especially in its articulation of the human relationship to the sacred.

In this perspective, it is not only the sacred which is perceived in terms of the world; the world too is perceived, thanks to the power of metaphor, in terms of the sacred. In regard to the conception of love in mystical literature, then, what this suggests is a simultaneous, indivisible perception of both worldly and spiritual eros. This places mystical literature into the category of humanistic literature in general, though as a distinctive tradition within it.

To read a work like the poetry of Hafiz without projecting *a priori* expectations derived from Sufi doctrine onto it, is to appreciate the perspective, characteristic to him, in which he saw all experience. This perspective is humanistic rather than religious in the restricted sense. Rumi's case is more complex. It may be said that it is more easy to categorise: the presence of Sufi doctrine in his poetry is unmistakable. Still, his poetry is more complex than this, if only because it is multi-layered. If one reads the *Mathnawi* as one might read literature, and not as a literary treatment of doctrine, one will notice features which are best understood in a literary perspective. One of these is the presence of more than one voice in the work. There is the voice within the stories. Then there is Rumi's authorial voice which imposes itself on the stories, interpreting them didactically, so as to ensure that the reader gets the right message—draws the right moral—from the tale. This makes the tales consciously allegorical. But the reader has the advantage of access not only to Rumi's instructional voice but to the logic of the tales themselves. He has the means to be entertained and edified by the symbolic and narrative structure of the stories. The sensibility in these stories is impressively wide-ranging. Not narrowly religious, they are amusing, touching, thought-provoking, and full of ribaldry and earthy humour.[6] At the same time, they are culturally Islamic, being interspersed by Qur'anic verses and anecdotes from Sufi predecessors. Thus, they operate at more than one level. And the act of reading, if it is to be an appropriate response, must likewise proceed on several levels at once.

There is no room in a short essay like this for detailed examples. Suffice it to reiterate the general point. The presence of literary imagination in mystical literature is not a mere appendix to its doctrinal aspect. It has a primary density and richness which is missed in an approach centred on theology or doctrine. Studies of this literature *qua* literature would be a major contribution to an understanding of world literature as a whole. It would also help highlight the fact that the subject material of human experience in a great tradition like that of Islam has a unity which does not lend itself to a rigid dichotomy of the religious and the secular. For better or worse, this dichotomy is a product of modern history. It is not an authentic reflection of primordial human cultures.

III

The preceding section has helped to highlight two facets of Sufism (or Islamic mysticism). One is its character as a specific tradition. The other is its basis in certain universal (existential) concerns characteristic of human life in society. These concerns overlap with the limiting facts of biology as well as of culture. They concern birth and death, body and mind, passion and reason, the manifold influences of society on the self (and the consequent search for one's 'true self'), love, disunion, and estrangement, hope, faith, and quest for the real. It is clear that there is a dualism, in all this: a dualism of the facts of natural and social life on the one hand, and the search for meaning on the other. For human beings seldom—or never—experience life without wanting to make sense of it. Culture is the source as well as the product of this quest for meaning. Religious cultures provide meaning in a form shaped by the human encounter with the sacred. Some of these cultures have historically developed into great civilisations. Islam, of course, is one of these, while Sufism is a strand within this historical civilisation. It has its defining concerns, its own vocabulary, and its doctrinal presuppositions. But it is also capable of being understood across cultures. In this susceptibility to migration beyond the barriers of organised faiths, languages, and social classes, its universality is palpable beneath the trappings of particularity.

It is appropriate, in this connection, to say a brief word about Ibn al-'Arabi. Among the theorists of Sufism, Ibn al-'Arabi is like a giant, who towers over everyone else. His thought is truly original, rejecting both Sunni and Shi'i traditionalism. He drew on Platonic, Neoplatonic, and gnostic ideas, and on traditions of Islamic esoteric thought; but he used all of these in his own way to form his own system—a system that is remarkable in more ways than one.

One of the remarkable features of Ibn al-'Arabi's thought is its sustained fusion between concept and image. He thinks logically and poetically at one and the same time. Each side feeds off the other. Unlike the Sufi poets (like Rumi), he is a master of discursive, analytic thought. Unlike the philosophers, who are masters of analytic thought, he knows the truth of imagination. Moreover, all this adds up to a scheme of thought which radically challenges the assumptions of orthodoxy. It is not only the theological incidentals of orthodoxy, but some of its central features, like its understanding of God, that he puts robustly into question.

We can refer, in passing, to only one aspect of his work. This has to do with the pluralism of religious consciousness, a thesis which is a central ingredient in his work. This thesis owes itself to the notions of symbolism and imagination—features, that is, of the poetics of religious experience.

What justifies pluralism of religious consciousness is Ibn al-'Arabi's conception of knowledge of the sacred. Knowledge does not involve correspondence of the mind with reality, but rather an imagination of the Real. It follows that knowledge of the sacred—religious consciousness—varies from one tradition to another.

Ibn al-'Arabi's overriding concern was with the unity or one-ness of reality. But this theme of oneness goes hand in hand with a recognition of the relativity—hence diversity—of human points of view on reality. Ultimately, reality remains unknowable. The idea of God, in Ibn al-'Arabi's way of thinking, is a symbol rather than an exact representation of ultimate reality. (We can detect the whole question of the relationship between word and real-ity—how language can 'refer' to what is outside it—buried in this proposition.) It is the form in which the Absolute makes itself known to man. Hence to know the divine one must know oneself. For there is always a form in which the Absolute becomes known to man. This aspect of 'appearing-to-man' is fundamental. One cannot really know reality except insofar as it is conceived by hu-man beings. Hence to know the divine (which is not an independent object but a relation) and to know the human es-sence are one and the same thing. In knowing the divine, one knows how one conceives of the divine.

From this idea there follows the relativity of all religious be-lief. Ibn al-'Arabi's thought is remarkable for its all-embracing acceptance of *all* religious points of view. Each nation or people, conceives of the Real in its own way. This imaginative charity of Ibn al-'Arabi reaches out even to idolatry. Just as in Latin Europe all roads were said to lead to Rome, in Ibn al-'Arabi's terms all images of God lead to the Absolute. An illustration of this view may be found in Ibn al-'Arabi's gloss on the story of Noah in the Qur'an. The traditional story of Noah is that he was sent by God, like all prophets, to warn people off their false gods—their idols—and to turn to the True God. Neglect of this message calls down calamity on the heedless, and so it is said to have done in the case of Noah's people. When they fail to heed his message, they are divinely punished. Now Ibn al-'Arabi gives an arresting, unortho-dox twist to this interpretation of the passage. He asserts the one-sidedness of both Noah and the condemned people. The idolaters were blind to the One behind the many. For this they were punished. However, Ibn al-'Arabi makes the rather subver-sive point that Noah's insistence on the One at the expense of the many was also one-sided. A total understanding must encompass

the One as well as the manifold of its self-disclosure. Hence those
famous lines, in which the heart encompasses myriads of forms:

> My heart has become capable
> of every form:
> A meadow for gazelles, a monastery for monks,
> A house of idols, the Ka'ba for the pilgrim,
> Tablets of the Torah, the corpus of the Qur'an.
> I follow the religion of love.
> Where its camels turn, there lies
> my religion, my faith.[7]

The poetry puts into graphic terms, concepts which belong to
Ibn al-'Arabi's notoriously difficult prose. This difficulty accentu-
ates a problem which bedevils studies of metaphysical thought in
general: an obliviousness, namely, to its political and cultural implications. It is all too common an experience to read expositions
of mystical literature which proceed as if such implications were
never there. But this is a gross omission. No metaphysical specula-
tion is innocent, in the last analysis, of a stance towards the world.

Although Ibn al-'Arabi's categories of thought move entirely
within the frame of esoteric or mystical thought—social or political issues could not have been more remote from his mind—the
ideas we just examined have implications, nevertheless, for the
politics of belief.

To illustrate this, it is sufficient to consider one of the consequences of the historical spread of Islamic culture from the Near
East to places like South Asia. The immigration of Arabian and
Iranian culture into this region stimulated a burst of cultural creativity (which was especially marked in the Mughal period). There
was a traffic between indigenous and immigrant symbols. In keeping with the principle of 'like attracts like', new traditions in poetry,
architecture, and the arts came into being.

The history of Indo–Islamic culture can be traced broadly at
two very different levels of society. One is that of the court and its
social environment. The other is that of folk religion, where Sufi
symbols and those from earlier Indian religious movements (like
bhakti), coalesced into new traditions. These traditions are commonly labelled as 'syncretic'. Orthodox *'ulama* periodically

castigate them for deviating from true Islamic norms. These judgements, which reject the identity of local Islam, are sometimes
internalised by local communities. As a result, apologists, anxious
to defend the local traditions against charges of 'un-Islamic' innovation, tend to underplay or rationalise the vernacular as
opposed to the Arabo–Persian ingredients of their traditions. This
phenomenon begs important questions.

As far as the poetry in these traditions is concerned, it is certain that 'syncretism' as a label will not do. The authors of this
poetry were not blenders: they were innovators. Their work deserves to be recognised in its own right, its own inner integrity.
The categories of 'Islamic' and 'non-Islamic', or for that matter,
Arabo–Persian and vernacular, are beside the point. They do not
illuminate the literature, but subject it, rather, to ideological polemic. This raises the important question of the meaning of
'Islamic' (and 'un-Islamic') in contexts like these. What is meant
by these terms? By what criteria are the 'Islamic' credentials of an
idea or practice determined? And by whom?

It is worth noting in this connection that while the Muslim
world was historically a scene of considerable polemic, in the
course of which accusations of heresy were commonly traded to
and fro, there was no one with the formal authority to pronounce
on true doctrine. There were, therefore, no institutionally defined
criteria by which correct belief could be sifted from incorrect
doctrine. The 'principles of faith' (*usul al-din*) which are said to
form the Islamic 'creed' are, in fact, principles of jurisprudence
consolidated through the informal consensus of scholars. In fact,
there was a wide variety of traditions of thought. One has only to
glance at the differences among the ways of thinking of traditionalists, theologians, philosophers, and mystical thinkers (like Ibn
al-'Arabi) to appreciate a phenomenal variety of points of view.

Of course, each sect or school of thought took it for granted
that its interpretation was the only true understanding of Islam.
In fact, it was not presented as an 'interpretation' (for which term,
in this general sense, there is in any case no Arabic equivalent).
For the relativity implied in this term is a modern conception.
Each school presented its doctrine as the truth, with a supporting

rationalisation, and a polemical refutation of its antagonists. But this is a very different matter from where (as in Christianity) there are institutional procedures for the formulation of true doctrine.

Moreover, the 'official' belief and practice in any tradition—whether *de facto* or *de jure*—is bound to differ from the reality on the ground. Muslim societies, with their historical and geographical span, are no exception to this rule. To realise this is to recognise the difference between speaking about Islam and speaking about Muslim societies. The religious life of Muslim societies is an organic aspect of their local and regional cultures. It is Islamic in as much as it constantly refers back to the paradigms and symbols associated with the events of the revelation and the life of the Prophet Muhammad. Each Muslim society nevertheless reflects its own unique bent of identity. As such, it cannot be reduced to any overlying abstraction.

Throughout the history of Islam, a pluriform rather than uniform culture has been characteristic of the reality of Muslim societies. This remains true of the modern Muslim world, except that the modern period has given a new lease of life, paradoxically, to the idea of uniformity. Two historical circumstances have contributed to this development. First, there has been a self-consciousness about Islam as a religio-cultural system. This self-consciousness came into its own only in the modern period. The debates and conflicts of the classical period were over substantive matters of law, jurisprudence, theology and philosophy, rather than over definitions of 'Islam'. Self- consciousness about Islam was in part a product of the Muslim world's encounter with the imperial powers of the modern West. Its reaction to these powers promoted a new consciousness of itself. This is often described nowadays as a resurgence or revival of Islam. But the reality is more subtle. What is now envisaged as an Islamic order is in fact a recombination of classical and modern symbols and conceptions. This is, of course, inevitable. And one of the results of this process is an *idea* of Islam—an idea which involved a heightened degree of self-consciousness; and which therefore produces a new kind of obsession with separating the 'Islamic' from the 'non-Islamic'.

After the dissolution of the empires, Islam came to serve a function equivalent to that of nationalism. This role has grown in importance with the abrupt collapse of once powerful ideologies like that of socialism. There has also been another transformation. The modern state has, at its disposal, far more instruments and mechanisms of social control than pre-modern governments, which lacked the means for centralised control over any but the smallest territories. Modern bureaucracies are more organised and specialised. The modern state has control over communications to a degree unthinkable in earlier eras. (This statement has to be qualified by reference to the globalisation of electronic communication now under way; but it does not negate the general point.) The modern state also has powerful means of controlling education (though education has seldom been immune, in human history, to being perverted into indoctrination). Lastly, modern societies, with their mass participation in politics, are susceptible to previously unknown heights of collectivisation. All this makes it easier for a state apparatus, or for anti-establishment movements, to project (and sometimes to enforce) mass conformity.

Modern calls for an 'Islamisation' of society—for purification of culture along Islamic lines—must therefore be understood against the background of the above-mentioned factors. Despite the novelty of these factors, however, contemporary ideological tensions in the Muslim world have clear antecedents in earlier history. Contrasting attitudes to regional Islam are a good example where modern factors come into play, but with clear precedents in history.

There has been a long-standing tension in much of Islamic history, between two broad outlooks. One of these, usually voiced by urban *'ulama*, is the outlook of traditionalism. The drive to orthodoxy involves the negative act of combating 'heresy', or *bid'a* ('innovation')—ideas or practices seen as 'alien' to Islam (as defined in this particular tradition). These ideas fell, historically, into two broad classes. One of these comprise learned traditions of thought, such as the philosophy inherited from the Greeks. The other class is that of popular religious culture. This generally includes oral literature, rites of passage, pilgrimages and festivals, devotion to holy figures (like *pir*s), music and dance as instruments of mystical ecstasy, rituals of healing, etc. What is generally called 'esoteric' Islam spans both ends of the spectrum. It gave rise, at one end, to highly speculative and abstract systems, accessible only to a learned elite. Popular Islam falls at the other end. However, popular forms of Islam were substantially influenced by the more learned writings. Thus, despite the idiosyncratic and obscure character of many of Ibn al-'Arabi's writings, they had a wide influence. Popular poetry and the collective practice of the *tariqa*s (mystical fraternities) were two of the vehicles through which philosophical ideas were transformed into collective archetypes and symbols accessible to the broader urban—and indeed, rural—population of pre-modern Islamic societies.

Ibn al-'Arabi's influence in this respect was especially pronounced. His works were studied by people with the ability and inclination to chase the taxing labyrinths of his thought. But more generally, his influence on popular Islam was probably indirect. In this connection, it is worth noting that the liberal—indeed, perhaps, latitudinarian—implications of Ibn al-'Arabi's thought has exact echoes in the tolerant variety of Islam in lands like the Indian subcontinent, exhibited in the preaching of Sufis (as opposed to conquest). Ibn al-'Arabi's contribution lies in providing a theoretical charter for the tolerant attitude (in the sense we are concerned with the present), whether this was conscious or unconscious.

Logically, pluralism poses a thorny dilemma in monotheistic societies. In polytheistic societies (like Hinduism), a pluralism of truth is implied in the very doctrine of polytheism. By contrast, monotheism has a built-in potential for monologism (the legitimacy of a single logic). However, a lot depends, in this respect, on how the sacred—the divine will—is believed to be knowable. And this is tantamount to the problem of the relationship between the word and reality. Does the word—the scriptural tradition, for instance—correspond directly to the real, as the names of physical objects are said to 'correspond' to objects, and as propositions of fact are said to 'correspond' with states of affairs in the world?

We can see how religious premises can involve, as they do in this case, very large intellectual questions. We also see how wide the scope of these questions has to be. They are no longer questions merely of religious belief. They concern man's relationship, in action or knowledge, to the world. They involve, therefore, questions of language, culture, and politics. Lastly, to see the relevance of these questions is to realise one of the colossal intellectual needs in the Muslim world today—the need, namely, for a theology with the intellectual wherewithal for taking up and exploring these questions. Such theology will require simultaneous mastery over the classical history of Islam and over almost every department of modern knowledge.

I intend to deal with these larger questions elsewhere. For the time being, however, let us return to the specific question of the problem of pluralism within a religious context, and Ibn al-'Arabi's contribution to this ideal. The role of creative imagination in religious belief—a thesis with which Ibn al-'Arabi is rightly identified, having given it a more elaborate and sustained formulation than anyone else in the classical history of Islam—was crucial in encouraging an appreciation of the varieties of religious experience. It must not be forgotten that Ibn al-'Arabi was first and foremost a psychologist of religious imagination. While his philosophy upheld unity of being, he was keenly sensitive to the empirics of imagination. Being a systematic thinker, he did not simply surrender, as mystical enthusiasts do, to the claims of mystical rapture. He analysed the religious imagination in the manner (speaking in modern terms) of a phenomenologist. The insights to which this led enriched the entire mystical tradition after him.

It will be of interest, while considering the question of popular Islam, to shift from Ibn al-'Arabi's abstract thought to the more accessible medium of narrative poetry. We are interested at this stage in whether narrative poetry in Islam offers exact counterparts, in its own terms, of Ibn al-'Arabi's theoretical ideas. We can do no better to this end than to turn again to Rumi. We do this in the next section.

IV

The passage in Rumi which is of utmost relevance to the issue
raised in the last section relates an imaginary episode. Moses, the
lawgiver, comes across a country peasant chatting to God in a personal way. He is shocked by what he hears:

> On the way Moses saw a shepherd
> saying: O God who chooses,
> where are you
> that I may serve you?
> That I may mend your shoes
> and comb your head.
> That I may wash your clothes
> and kill the lice on you
> and serve you milk,
> O revered one!
> That I may kiss your little hand
> and massage your little foot.
> And come night-time,
> sweep your sleeping-place.
> I sacrifice
> all my goats to you.
> In your remembrance
> are all my cries and sighs.
>
> In this way the shepherd talked
> foolishly.
>
> Moses said: For whom is this meant, fellow?
>
> He said: For He who made us. He due to whom
> this earth and sky came into our view.
> Moses said: You have backslided,
> wretched one.
> It is not a Muslim you have come to be
> but an infidel.
> What idle chatter is this?
> What blasphemy?
> What raving?
> Stuff your mouth!
> The smell of your blasphemy

has made the world stink.
It has torn the robe of faith.
Shoes and stockings are good for you.
How can they be right for the Sun?
If you don't stop these words in your throat,
a fire will come to scorch the land.
If there is no fire here,
what then is this smoke?
Why has your soul gone black?
Why are you spurned?
If God knows all, why
this doting talk and familiarity?
A fool's friendship is enmity;
the great Lord is not in need of this prayer.
To whom do you say this—
your uncle, you think?
Are body and its needs attributes of the Glorious One?
Only he who is growing drinks milk.
He who needs feet is the one
who puts on shoes.

Or if these words are for His servant,
of whom God said: He is I
and I myself am he.
Of whom He said: I was sick
and you didn't visit me;
I too became ill, not just he.
He who came to be seeing
and hearing by Me—
for that servant too,
all this is foolishness.
To speak without reverence
to the chosen one of God
makes the heart wither
and blackens the page.
If you called a man Fatima,
though man and woman are one species,
he will want to kill you,
though he may be kind and forbearing and gentle.
Fatima is praise to a woman;
to a man it is the stab of a spear.
Hand and foot are fitting to us—

to the Holy God, a blemish.

He did not beget nor was He begotten—
this is for Him. He is the Creator
of begetter and begotten.
Birth belongs to whatever has a body,
whatever is born is on this side of the river.
It is of the becoming and the decaying and the despicable.

The shepherd said: O Moses, you have shut my mouth
and with remorse scorched my soul.
He tore his clothes and heaved a sigh,
turned to the desert
and went his way.

There was a revelation from God to Moses:

You have parted my servant from me.
Did you come to unite, or did you come to sever?
Step not into severance, so far as you can.
Of all the things the most loathsome to me is divorce.
To each I have given a way of acting,
To each a way of speaking.
To him it is praise, to you a fault.
To him it is honey, to you poison.
I care not for purity or pollution,
dullness or cleverness.
Among Hindus the idiom of Hind is right;
Among Sindhis the idiom of Sindh is right.

I am not made holy by their praise.
It is they who turn pure and pearl-scattering.
I look not to tongue and speech,
rather to the inward state.
I look into the heart, whether it is humble,
no matter if the words be un-humble.
For the heart is the essence; speech an accident.
Well then, the accident is secondary,
the essence is the point.[8]

We should note here, first, the contrast between the voices of Moses and the shepherd. Moses speaks with the stern precision of a lawgiver, a judge. He rebukes the shepherd for his artless speech, his colloquial ardour. In the process, he passes easily into speaking on behalf of God the Judge. While he speaks *about* God, he seems so certain of the standards of divine judgement, that he talks as if in the voice of God. (Indeed, the figure of Moses here stands for all religious officials—'men of cloth' as it were). Again, he speaks in the learned terms of a theologian. (This is, of course, anachronistic, but in a poetic conceit this hardly matters.) He teaches, scolds, denounces, with the indignation proper to a guardian of orthodoxy. His judgements rush forward in a torrent, carrying the weight of authoritative learning. They fall, heavy with a scholar's erudition, on the frail shoulders of the peasant. The impact is plainly traumatic.

The shepherd and Moses are both talkative characters. But their speech is not symmetrical, and this is true in more than one way. The shepherd's words are simple not only in being free of theology; the syntax too is simpler. An initial, direct question—'where are you?'—is followed by a series of what are in effect purposive clauses, statements of intent. His imagination, aflame with tender affection, thinks up gestures of customary etiquette of hospitality. They rest securely on the twin basis of tradition and personal sincerity. The force of this sincerity rules out scruples over the guest's royal status. The conversational tone of the shepherd's speech is in marked contrast to solemn speech. It is far removed from the tone appropriate to a subject's petition to his sovereign. It is an intimate overture, seductively caressing, passing into uninhibited gestures of physical, tactile devotion. Where the law of Moses is all propriety and restraint, the shepherd's imagination is only too personal and intimate.

Both, again, speak with unshakeable self-assurance. But Moses' sense of certainty flows from the authority of what he knows; the shepherd's innocent self-confidence comes from the authenticity of his passion.

It is also interesting to note the contrast in images of space. Moses' speech encompasses the universe ('the Sun') and (as in the Qur'an), nations or communities (doomed when they transgress). Implicitly, Moses' terms invoke the library of the '*alim*, the learned scholar. The shepherd's 'space' is his homestead, with all its familiarity and warmth. It is on a scale suited to intimate exchanges of speech and act. The objects invoked are basic items of food, clothing, and shelter. In keeping with this scale of space and furniture, the imagery is elementally domestic, while the vocabulary is free from abstract concepts or dialectic.

Into this homely idiom the scholastic and moral vocabulary of Moses intrudes with something of the force of a bulldozer. His diction is more complex. At its simplest it denounces; at its most subtle it is a disquisition on the person of the Creator. Between these two forms it takes in legislative pronouncement, prophetic warning of doom, moral sermonising, and instruction by analogy. The complexity of his diction matches the symbolic complexity of the figure itself. It would be wrong to say that Rumi depicts Moses as an altogether unsympathetic figure; though, to appreciate this, one needs to know the elevated status that the *Mathnawi* gives him in his several appearances in the text as a whole. Nevertheless, his portraiture here is, in a word, ironic. It sharpens our sense of paradox. Moses is not a mere pedant. He communicates the intellectual wisdom of a sacred tradition. But, precisely because it is the wisdom of a learned tradition, it has limitations. There is mastery over argument, nuance, analogy; there are insights into things human and divine, the mysteries of the Godhead. But a mind fortified by all this fails to fathom the passion of a dedicated heart.

Paradox is built into Moses' sermon. Even as he expounds on God's transcendence, His freedom from human wants and limitations, he makes reference to the opposite tradition in Islam—the tradition of immanence. This tradition identifies the divine with the human essence—'he is I, and I myself am He'. The plight of the humble, the poor and the sick, become a divine affliction, an offence to the divine order of things. This does not negate Moses' thesis of transcendence. He makes the reference consciously, insisting that it does not invalidate its argument. But if these two themes are not contradictory, they do mark a poetic counterpoint.

As in contrapuntal music, the presence of more than one voice in a poetic text introduces several, at times confrontative, motifs. Logically, Moses' speech is a single, consistent argument. Thematically, however, it is, despite itself, multi-tonal.

The third voice—that of God—is a voice of judgement, saying, in effect: judge not lest ye be judged. It issues a forthright rebuke. The rhetorical question—whether Moses was sent to join or to separate—puts his very credentials, momentarily, into question. The clarification which follows stresses the individual complexion of cultures. To each person his own experience; to each nation its specific tongue. God's point of view is Olympian (or, we might say, Sinaian). It sees everything, foreclosing nothing. He stands majestically above the babble of tongues and the multitude of forms. He sees forms for what they are, being rather on the look-out for what lies beneath. To Him, the beat of an ardent heart is audible through the rant of indelicate speech. Rules which hold outside a sanctuary quickly lose their point inside. The poetry of love leaps easily over barriers of form and tradition.

While the words attributed to God carry the authority and finality proper to them, they suggest intimacy rather than formal majesty. This comes across in two ways: the arresting experience of hearing the divine voice in the vernacular Persian as opposed to Arabic, the language of the Qur'an; and the self-reference which occurs several times in the singular first person pronoun (as opposed to the 'royal' plural). The various voices weave together in an atmosphere of intimate exchange as opposed to formal pronouncement. A certain continuity between man and God is suggested, mitigating the vertical distance of transcendence.

What the passage underlines is the diversity, the inescapable limitations, the irreducibly personal quality of all religious experience. It is of undoubted literary interest in itself, but my purpose in remarking on it here is wider. By opposing the ideal of personal authenticity to the strictures of law and theology, Rumi's narrative raises a larger question. What are the different epistemologies—theories of knowledge—responsible, in the Islamic context, for this and rival points of view on the human relationship to the sacred?

The passage in itself endorses certain values which we have already noted. It upholds the claims of personal passion and expression against those of scholastic and theological normativism. Implicit in this is a very important social statement. The story champions the right to speech on the part of the socially marginalised. They are entitled, the story declares, to their own dialect or language—their own culture, as we would nowadays say. It champions the vernacular of the heart against the *lingua franca* of scholastic theology. And all this is linked together and to the centre of the *Mathnawi* by the theme of inner authenticity, which gives pride of place to the heart over the tongue.

But beyond this there are questions of history as well as philosophy. What developments led to Rumi's position? To what rival positions, carrying their own historical background, was it a reaction? This is the historical question. The philosophical question involves assumptions about knowledge and meaning which lie behind various interpretations of faith in the Islamic context, including the ones which we have been exploring in Ibn al-'Arabi and Rumi.

I have already referred, in passing, to these general issues. In the next section I wish to elaborate on them. Having done this, however, we will be obliged to press on to a yet broader issue.

Questions of seminal importance in Islam can scarcely concern Islam alone. Islam is not a *sui generis* phenomenon. As one of the great civilisations of the world, it reflects, in its own way, riddles characteristic of the human estate on earth. To study one civilisation is to become aware, by implication, of others. The problems of interpretation we have been dealing with here, however specific they may seem to Islam, are not confined to it. They have a way of crossing borders—not only borders between faiths, so that the study of comparative religion is, in the last analysis, essential for the study of a particular religion; but also borders between civilisations, so that ultimately even 'religion' is a territory with indistinct borders. In commenting on the opening passage of Rumi's *Mathnawi*, we tried to observe this principle by suspending all mystical, indeed religious, presuppositions in favour of the wider field of human psychology and culture. It is only fitting, therefore, that the essay should conclude on this note, though it need hardly be said that it can only glance at, rather than venture into these wider vistas.

V

The history of Islam begins, of course, with the revelatory event in the life of the Prophet Muhammad. We have already remarked on the significance of the fact that this was an event, and hence an open, evolving process, not a closed, finished system of ideas. Even though the Qur'an as a book testifies only indirectly to this process—for the oral event lies concealed behind the book—it carries many traces of it. It shows the impact of historical incidents on the content of the preaching. And it reflects an evolutionary element in the measures regulating the community concurrently with changes in the Prophet's relationship with his opponents in Mecca and Medina, and with other groups, principally the Jews in Medina. To a great extent the Qur'an, when analysed chronologically, is a historical record. It shows the evolving fortunes of the Prophet's followers, who began as a small, loose band of individuals in Mecca, inspired by the Prophet's charisma and bound to him, therefore, by ties of personal loyalty. From this stage the movement grew, after the Prophet's migration to Medina and his gaining of support there, into the beginnings of a community with a distinct identity.

The charismatic nature of the Prophet's leadership was all important. Not till long after his death did it come to be (in Max Weber's words) 'routinised': codified into a law, with elements of theological doctrine. What the Qur'an presents are powerful symbols of human existential concerns—the meaning of life and death, the whence and wherefore of things (origination and destiny), the bond between the being of man and the being of all things. There is, no doubt, a body of regulations designed to organise domestic and social relations among the Prophet's followers. And there are pronouncements, therefore, on sexual relations, transactions of goods, inheritance of wealth, and penalties for transgressions. These, however, bear the clear stamp of history. Moreover, the injunctions—some of which are given in fairly detailed terms while others appear in only more general terms—are part of the more general context of the moral vision of the Qur'an.

On the whole, therefore, the Qur'an is an ethical, not a legal text. This is one of the reasons why Muslim jurists in the classical Islamic age had to evolve legal systems afresh, though they attempted to relate these to the Qur'an through various conventions of deductive interpretation. Even then, conventions of authority additional to the Qur'an became essential. This general or open character of the Qur'an's pronouncements is closely related to the charismatic character of the Prophet's authority. This is evident in two broad respects.

First, the Prophet gave responses to situations as they arose and called for his decision. This process usually involved a search, on his part, for the right answer. The process of search often involved consultation with the notables around him; and it always involved consultation with the inner voice guiding him. But apart from his personal role, we have to note one of the consequences of the fact that the revelation was essentially a call to a moral life. Laws derive their point and purpose from the ethical impulses of which they are an embodiment. This can clearly be seen from a contemporary phenomenon. When, nowadays, specific laws appear unjust, anachronistic, or pointless, these problems prove themselves intractable to textual interpretation (of the Constitution or of Common Law precedents). They compel recourse, instead, to first principles: to philosophical considerations, social functions, and political premises. In the absence of this recourse, a legal system becomes self-enclosed, arbitrary, and fossilised—in a word, irrational.

When the Arabs conquered cities of the Near East in the decades following the Prophet's death, they did not think of replacing the old-established traditions and institutions of the ancient empires—the Roman and the Persian—which they had supplanted. Nor, of course, could they have done so, had they so wished, as they had yet to develop their own counterparts to these institutions. The Qur'an provided them with a general sense of their place in the world. Pre-Islamic traditions also provided long-last-ing standards of behaviour and codes of honour. Only gradually did these legacies combine with cultural traditions of the conquered lands, adapting them and becoming adapted to them in the process.

At the beginning, therefore, legal practice followed traditions in the cities of the conquered lands. However, with the growth of the Muslim population—a population of rulers, administrators, landowners and merchants—the evolution of a recognisably Islamic order became a necessity. It was necessary to introduce a measure of ideological unity in what was, socially and culturally, a heterogeneous population. It was essential to have standards or criteria by which the Muslims could be tangibly distinguished from the followers of other persuasions. What was needed were the makings, on a collective level, of what we nowadays call identity.

The Christian Church had provided a definition for Christianity, well beyond the broad ethic of the Gospels, by giving it a creed. Muslim society was apt to give a corresponding emphasis to law, i.e. the *shari'a* (of which, it must be remembered, 'law' is an imperfect translation). For the *shari'a* encompasses moral and religious norms as much as rules of behaviour; and these rules, moreover, encompass 'private' as well as 'public' conduct. What must also be remembered, however, is not only that the *shari'a* evolved historically, but that this history bears the marks of a protracted struggle, waged on many fronts, between very different and competing mentalities.

For over a hundred and fifty years after the Prophet's death, judges in various urban centres gave their rulings by relying on their conscience, their intellectual judgement, ethical intuition, and pragmatic calculation. As a conscious search for an Islamic justification for these procedures gathered ground, appeal to Qur'anic ideals became all-important. Nonetheless, there was not a single group which could define these ideals, and their practical implications, on behalf of society as a whole. The attempt was pursued severally by individual scholars and teachers in the cities concerned. Inevitably, therefore, there was a strong, continuing reliance by these individuals on personal analysis and judgement.

This dependence on personal reasoning was challenged by

individuals who eventually coalesced into a campaigning movement. They insisted on the supremacy, in place of personal
judgement, of the text of traditions derived from the Prophet.
This text, and that of the Qu'ran, ought, in their view, to override
personal inquiry and judgement. In essence, therefore, the position of the *ahl al-hadith* (People of the Hadith), as this movement
was called, was authoritarian, appealing, as it did, to the binding
authority of tradition.

The lawyers, whom this movement attacked, could hardly ar-
gue against this appeal to the sayings and practices of the Prophet.
Nonetheless, they did not surrender to its implications against
the use of reason. They argued that an indiscriminate reliance on
Prophetic tradition was vulnerable to a very wide margin of fabri-
cation and arbitrariness. Their criticisms led, in turn, to a
methodology for sifting between traditions according to their
degree of likely authenticity, ascertained by reference to the sound-
ness of their transmission. With this development, the outlook of
the People of Hadith was set on a course of victory over that of
the lawyers who had opposed them.

Other elements were, over time, added to this point of view.
One was a rejection of the rationalism of the school of thought
known as the Mu'tazila. This historically important school maintained that the Qu'ran was not part of the divine essence but a
created phenomenon, and that human beings were capable of
rationally recognising right and wrong, and free to choose between them. The People of the Hadith found this view
unacceptable. Scripture—the text of the Qur'an and the Prophetic
traditions—ought to have, in their view, a literal supremacy over
human reason, will, and behaviour. The Mu'tazila had tried to
assimilate the concept of the divine into a vision of a rational universe. Revelation, to them, was the expression of a more
fundamental reason. A recent textbook of Islamic history summarises this view aptly: 'Revelation could supply details, complete,
confirm, or complement reason, but no truths unknown,
unknowable or inconsistent with the dictates of reason could be
revealed.'[9]

This idea of the sovereignty of reason was unacceptable to the traditionalists. It should be noted that what was at stake in these debates was not only the question of what the universe is like but of what way of life is to be regarded as legitimate. There is a sense in which metaphysical doctrines—doctrines about what is ultimately real—are not about what exists but about how human beings are to relate to what exists. Islamic rationalism promoted the life of reason in society. Islamic traditionalism advocated submission of one's will to the scriptural or textual tradition (conceived as the will of God) as the only legitimate basis of social order.

Rationalism, here mentioned in connection with the Mu'tazila, brings to mind two other important schools of thought, namely, Hellenistic philosophy and Ismailism. Hellenistic philosophy was the tradition of philosophical thought originating from the work of the great masters of Ancient Greece, notably Plato and Aristotle. When the ideas of these great thinkers were received by intellectuals in the Near East, they underwent a development and transformation. They were eagerly studied and preserved—but also, through commentaries and reflection, interpreted and adapted. The result, which was like a central current depositing its silt and fertilising the soil of the Near East, but also receiving tributaries from it in the process, was Hellenistic philosophy. This philosophy influenced intellectual life in medieval society, whether Jewish, Christian or Islamic. In the Muslim world, philosophers like al-Farabi, Ibn Sina (Avicenna) and Ibn Rushd (Averroes) were wholehearted followers of what they saw as the universal science of reason. They found in it an assured road to truth. It opened up horizons of the mind, by comparison with which the way of religion seemed to them intellectually all too parochial and limited. Still, they were obliged to make sense of religion through the very concepts and terminology of philosophy. In this way, they tried to reconcile their own commitment to rational inquiry with the plain fact that the mass of society would always need to subscribe unquestioningly to religious doctrine and law. By the same token, they hoped to reconcile the religious leaders of society to the presence of philosophy in their midst.

Although formulations of the relationship between philosophy and religion differed amongst the various philosophers in detail and nuance, two themes stand out. One was the recognition that the rigorous inquiry and objectivity which philosophy entails, is attainable only by a few. Society as a whole, however, needed to be held together by myth. (This was the quintessentially Platonic view.) Above all, the means to happiness in this world and the next lay in faithful adherence to the divine law.

In the ideal city, philosophers and the society would respect and tolerate each other. This was not just a matter of condescending forbearance on the part of the philosophers. Most of the philosophers were inclined to see in the principles of religious faith the same truth as that attained through philosophy (or science—for these two had not yet become separated). The difference was that in religion these truths were presented in an imaginative garb—in allegories and parables—which called other faculties of the mind (like the affective) into play, and were thus more likely to seize the imagination and win the allegiance of the collective mind.

As might be expected, interest in philosophical ideas was a subject of considerable controversy. Naturally, the traditionalist school had no truck with it: they were opposed not only to philosophy, which was seen as a foreign science, for it had not originated in Arabic, nor among Muslims. (These two criteria were treated as jointly paramount.) They were also vigorously opposed to theology, which is the intellectual articulation of principles accepted on faith. To the traditionalists, a subordination of the human will to the literal text of the religious tradition was the sole overriding imperative.

More than two hundred years after the first translations into Arabic of Greek works of philosophy and science—a task in which Jews and Christians were centrally involved—Abu Hamid al-Ghazali mounted an elaborate, learned, and withering attack on philosophy from the viewpoint of the religious tradition. His work heralded the consolidation of Sunni orthodoxy. The position defined by Ghazali was broader than that of the People of the Hadith. It signalled a partial acceptance of theology and mysticism, topics which the early traditionalists had rejected. But it was also clear about what was to be excluded: namely philosophy, the rationalism of the Mu'tazila, and not least, Ismailism. Against the latter, Ghazali deployed all his talent for polemic—a fact which shows the popular appeal of Ismaili ideas and ideals throughout the formative centuries of Islam. The importance of Ismaili ideas in the formative process of Islamic thought has been all but obliterated from orthodox accounts of history. Indeed, it could be argued that some of Ghazali's salient notions were coloured or influenced by Ismaili esotericism. For enmity is a form of intimacy. In wrestling closely against something, one wrestles against it in one's own being. In the process, one's outlook is bound to be penetrated by the very thing one seeks to fight and exclude.

In any case, the point to be emphasised is that what many textbooks on Islam assume to be the standard definition of Islam is by and large an uncritical assumption. It assumes an orthodoxy when, in fact, the orthodox definition was the outcome of a long historical process. This process was a struggle, in which many intellectual actors who had once been so prominent on the stage were now treated as marginal. This is why it is ultimately unhelpful to ask the question what Islam 'is'. It is far more illuminating to ask how various interpretations of Islam came to be what they are, in specific times and places. Nor is this solely a matter of setting the historical record straight. To recognise that Islamic thought had possibilities in many directions, and that it was by historical accident that it came to be treated as a settled body of timeless truths, is to create the possibility of a renewed openness. For history in the hands of an antiquarian is one thing; in the hands of an historical actor it is something else altogether.

To return to philosophy: Ghazali's attack on philosophy drew a spirited rejoinder, well after his death, from the philosopher Averroes, writing in Andalus. Ultimately, however, neither Ghazali's nor Averroes' books, both of which were—and remain—unreadable by anybody but a virtuoso of classical dialectic, was socially decisive. It was the exclusion of philosophy, and of the rational sciences in general, including esoteric philosophy—ranging from early Ismaili thought to Ibn al-'Arabi—from the *orthodox madrasa*s or colleges, and the resulting *de facto* institutionalisation of a particular definition of Islam, which influenced the picture of Islam which still lives on today.

Averroes was the last figure in the Aristotelian philosophical tradition which had flourished so well in the Muslim world. His work, which fell into oblivion in the Muslim world, was eagerly studied by a group of scholars in Paris and elsewhere in Europe who came to be known as Latin Averroists. There, Averroes' ideas fuelled a lively controversy and debate, forcing Thomas Aquinas to forge a doctrinal system which was religiously conservative in comparison. It presented the central axioms of Christianity as the summit of the exertions of natural reason. This system became the cornerstone of intellectual Catholicism.

A new chapter was inaugurated in the history of philosophy, following the rise of modern science, with Immanuel Kant's powerful attack on the metaphysical traditions which the Ancient Greeks and their Muslim, Jewish, and Christian successors had developed. After Kant and his successors, it is no longer possible to read classical or medieval philosophy without finding grave and fundamental flaws in it. But this continuing development and debate by-passed the Muslim world, where the philosophical tradition was subordinated to religious and mystical thought. In the latter domain, there was a considerable efflorescence, especially in Iran. The rupture in the history of philosophy has had the consequence, however, that when modern philosophical ideas entered the Muslim lands after contact with Europe, they were not in a state of dialogue or debate with the religious vision of Islam. Secular philosophy and religious learning thus followed different paths, as if guided by the maxim 'never the twain shall meet'. Religious knowledge is conceptualised very differently—as something already given, and awaiting mastery rather than creation—from the way philosophy, science, and the secular disciplines need, by their very nature, to be understood. Not the least consequence of this state of affairs is the absence in the Muslim world today of what was mentioned above: a philosophy of religion which could relate the new knowledge of the universe and human nature we have at our disposal today, with the religious history of Islam. The tradition itself is lacking, and absent, therefore, are the minds which can grapple simultaneously, and at the highest level of competence, with both these domains.

I should now like to complete these comments on classical Islamic history by a word on the important topic of Ismailism.

In speaking about 'Ismailism', one has to be careful, as with 'Islam', to make relevant distinctions and qualifications. The suffix 'ism' may suggest a uniform body of doctrines, whereas in fact, apart from allegiance to the Ismaili Imamate, the thought-forms, temperaments, and intellectual calibre of Ismaili authors differ widely. Secondly, the same suffix, with its suggestion of a self-contained doctrinal system, implies a sealed compartment, as it were, within the intellectual history of Islam. Nothing could be further from the truth. The issues with which Ismaili authors were concerned were the same as those which exercised the minds of other Muslims. The frameworks which were available to them—broadly speaking, the scriptural and the philosophical traditions—were the same. The challenge to understand each of these traditions in terms of the other confronted Ismaili intellectuals in the same way as others in the Muslim world.

Having said this, it must also be said that the Ismaili vision of the world in the formative period of Islamic history—roughly, the first four centuries, which includes the best of the Fatimid period—was a remarkably coherent one. In the hands of its more outstanding exponents, it was also highly original. It was clear in what it encompassed and what it eschewed. It rejected the traditionalist solution to the problem of jurisprudence which relied, in the last analysis, on the consensus of the *'ulama*. But this again, was not a simple reflection of sectarian division between 'Sunni' and 'Shi'a'. Thus, Fatimid Ismaili thinkers and the Mu'tazila had more in common with each other than either of them had with the People of Hadith, though in other respects their positions were profoundly different. The same may be said of Fatimid thinkers and the students of Plato and Aristotle mentioned above.

The history of Ismaili thought as such is not directly relevant to the subject of this essay. I mention it here with two purposes in mind. One is to take note of it in the context of the whole enterprise of rationalism, whose adherents tried to understand the world as a rational whole. The other is to illustrate a point about the relation between reason and the sense of the sacred in human culture which does happen to be of direct relevance to the theme of this essay.

The rationalism is especially pronounced in writers, particularly of eastern Iran, in the Fatimid period. In common with the Mu'tazila and the philosophers, these writers were strongly drawn to the intellectual attractions of philosophy. At the same time, however—and quite unlike the philosophers—they were the intellectual vanguards of a broad social and popular movement combining religious, political, and cultural aims in an all-encompassing vision. In short, Ismaili writers were not individual intellectuals but rather, ideologues of a movement. Such a movement needs more than ideas. It requires a world-view—one, however, which is not only philosophical but embraces a sociopolitical ideal. Furthermore, world-views prove credible only when they appear to correspond with the realities of the world. Conversely, the realities of society appear as legitimate only when they are explained in terms of a view of the world as a whole. Earnest as Fatimid authors were in pursuit of intellectual life, it was part of a social, religious, and political mission. Hence the view of the world which they promulgated was a comprehensive one, in which a cosmology, a system of religious guidance, and a social order were all fused into one.

The Fatimid authors did not agree with one another on all issues, and it is impossible, therefore, to speak of them as a collectivity. One of the more outstanding among them was Abu Ya'qub al-Sijistani.[10] On Sijistani's philosophy, I wish to make four observations here. One has to do with the aspect of his thought which merits being called 'rationalist'. The next two points refer to concepts which follow from this rationalism. The fourth observation will lead us beyond the rationalism itself to the relation between reason and the sense of the sacred.

Sijistani's rationalism lay in his conviction that (as with the Mu'tazila and the philosophers) the universe was a rational order. Once this premise was accepted, its proponents, whether in the Islamic, Christian, or Jewish worlds, were all confronted by the question: how is the religious or scriptural tradition to be accounted for *in terms* of the universal, objective, rational order? Paul Walker, the author of the monograph just cited, summarises Sijistani's position in this regard as follows:

> Whereas ordinary Muslims found their sources solely and exclusively in the singular scripture that formed the Qur'an and in the surviving record of the words and deeds of its prophet, Sijistani ... required a far more complete set of roots. What explains religion and faith, for them, must also explain everything else. The transcending intellectual reality that the Qur'an reflects ... must contain a truth so encompassing that all things and all parts of knowledge belong to it and under it.[11]

This ultimate order, of which the revealed laws are but one expression, is 'a world that can only be explored intellectually'.[12]

There are two other ideas here which are worth analysing. One is the concept of what the passage just cited calls 'roots'. The other is a methodology for journeying from the branches, as it were, to the roots.

The notion of 'roots' follows from the premise that revelation and law—the whole realm of religious symbols, in fact—is a *representation* of the ultimate order of being. It follows that the pursuit of knowledge or enlightenment calls for a procedure for tracing the representation back to its radical origin. (The word 'radical' is meant here in its etymological sense, which refers to 'root'.) In Sijistani this procedure (as with many other Ismaili authors in particular, but more generally, other Muslim writers also) is named *ta'wil*.

The term *ta'wil*, commonly translated as 'interpretation', is associated with the dualism of the outer and the inner, which was a hallmark of Ismaili thought. The relation between *ta'wil* and the dualism of the apparent and the real is one of mutual implication. The dualism of appearance and reality implies, as its corollary, a process of uncovering or penetration. Conversely, this operation makes sense only when appearances are not everything. This simple, logical formula is of far-reaching significance.

The Ismaili texts of this period, like the works of other writers such as Avicenna, exhibit *ta'wil*, as it were, in action. They take passages from the Qur'an, the Hadith, or (among the Shi'a) the teachings of the Imams, and gloss them for their 'inner' meanings. However, it is only too easy to interpret this anti-dogmatic procedure dogmatically. What is ultimately significant is not *what* meanings are found to lie 'behind' specific passages, but *that* they are understood in this manner. The very notion of symbolism, which goes with what might be called the plenitude of meaning, are no less significant than what the symbols are thought to 'symbolise'.

This point bears elaboration. What is commonly called allegorical interpretation tends to substitute a meaning (say Y) for another meaning (X). From a series of such interpretations, one may derive a code, giving automatic access from concepts in one column (marked *zahir*) to their supposed equivalents in another column (marked *batin*). The operative assumption here is that an individual term 'has' another meaning besides its obvious one; and that this other (singular) meaning can be known or shown once and for all, making it possible for one to say: 'the real meaning of X is Y.' But this 'is' here marks a very problematic equation.

In what sense does X mean Y? We have reason to surmise that when a man is nicknamed a lion he is probably brave or courageous; and that when he is nicknamed a dog he is probably vile (though why a dog—that 'much-maligned creature' as Dr Johnson pityingly called him—should have earned such a stigma in most cultures known to us is a puzzling question in itself). Such automatic transfer of a word to its metaphorical correlate is, however, the sign of a withered metaphor. For once a definite term (Y) is substituted for another definite term (X), the second term becomes superfluous. This is another way of saying that the essence of a metaphor is not meaning, but a *relationship* between meanings.

What is of enduring importance in the symbolic mode is a continual *creation* of meaning. That is, the specific meanings predicted reflect a specific context. The spirit of linguistic exploration is, however, a constant. We may put it this way: what is really important is to interpret the drive to interpret; to note the spirit of the very idea of seeking the spirit beneath the letter. By doing this, we keep the metaphorical domain alive; whereas when the symbol is definitively translated into a concept, the metaphor dies. Between a literalism which rejects metaphor, and a literalism which pays lip-service to it, there is, in the end, very little to choose.

With these considerations we arrive at the very heart of what is meant by the poetics of religious experience. Etymologically, the term 'poetics' implies a making, a creativity. In the context of religious experience, as we have seen, the creativity is in the symbolic process. Symbolic language carries what Paul Ricoeur calls a 'surplus of meaning'. The relationship of the symbolic process and intellectual or philosophical analysis is very specific. In Ricoeur's words, 'the symbol donates thought.' This unfolding of thought from image is a never-ending process. It is a continuous creativity, where one form supersedes another in march with life's onward-bound journey, personal as well as collective.

The bond between myth or symbol on the one hand, and conceptual or analytic thought on the other, is full of inner tension. This very tension, however, is a fount of creativity. Where critical thought loses touch with the symbolic mode, it yields knowledge without inspiration. On the other hand, critical thought has the valuable function of preventing mythical thought from being taken literally. Under the guidance of a critical interpretation, we learn not to take stories of creation, sacred figures, and sacred cosmologies literally. We do not equate them with the findings of the natural or social sciences. To this extent, science combats myth. At the same time, we learn to see in these stories, frameworks for a meaning and ethics of existence.

Sijistani's thought is but one example of this bond between existence and thought. Other examples can be found as readily from other civilisations. But within the intellectual history of Islam, what Sijistani's thought represents is a form of intellectual esotericism. This tradition was one of the many rich expressions of the search, in these civilisations, for the underlying bond between faith and intellect.

The 'roots' implied in the concept of *ta'wil* cannot be summed up in monological propositions. An intuitive recognition of this point seems to have been already present in the period we are considering. An example is the statement of the Fatimid theologian Hamid al-Din al-Kirmani that behind the *batin* there lies yet another *batin*. This extra term keeps the first *batin* from becoming fixed once and for all, as a closed formula. As Ibn al-'Arabi also remarked, there is no point at which the knower ('*arif*) ever comes to a stop.[13]

The idea of a bond between existential symbolism and reflective thought can be taken one step further. The terminology we have employed here is modern. However, the insight is age-old. In order to see this, we could paraphrase what has just been said in terms which belong to scriptural or prophetic discourse. The crucial concept here is that of idolatry. The critique of idolatry is a prophetic critique *par excellence.*

The concept of idolatry has rich ramifications of meaning. To appreciate these, we must take the notion itself metaphorically rather than literally. In essence, idolatry stands for a *negation of life.* The scriptural objection to idolatry is the fact that idols are unseeing, unhearing, and mute—in a word, lifeless. In contrast to the dead object, true divinity is synonymous with life.

Earlier we noted the quality of the revelation as a living event. We also noted that in the course of the search for an Islamic basis for the social order the Qur'an, along with the words of the Prophet, was adopted as a scriptural corpus. As a book, the Qur'an embodies the event of the revelation. But, by virtue of being a book, it is a representation of that event, and obviously not the event itself, with its motility, its evolutionary flow through the two decades or so of the Prophet's active preaching in Mecca and Medina.

Sensitive minds in subsequent history, recalling the revelation and the life of the Prophet, were aware of this paradox of nearness and distance, the directness of personal encounter and the indirectness of reported testimony. It is interesting, in this connection, to note a reported remark of the Shi'i Imam Ja'far al-Sadiq about different degrees of knowledge of the Qur'an, to the effect that there are degrees of acquaintance or encounters with the

Qur'an of people who, even with the distance of time, hear it as if it were being revealed to them there and then.[14] This remark is immensely rich in its implications. It registers a quest for the living event behind the text. By celebrating personal encounter over second-hand testimony, it promotes the word over its incarnation in the text.

The contrast between the living event and the text which, admittedly, is a testimony to life, but also susceptible to a separation from living history, can be put in terms of a central duality: the Book and the Person. Ja'far al-Sadiq's remark was no doubt meant in support of the Shi'i doctrine of the Imamate, where the living Imam is expected to make the text come to life through the historical, life-enhancing act of interpretation. The same polarity finds voice in other terms. One example is the Platonic archetype of the Perfect Man in Sufism. For a dramatisation of a contrast between a representation of life and the formalism of a relic, we turn again to an anecdote in Rumi.

The story tells, in undertones of blunt humour, of Bayazid, the famous Sufi hero, on his way to Mecca for the pilgrimage. On the way he meets an old Sufi master (a *shaykh*) who, noticing his baggage, asks him his destination. On hearing the reply, the *shaykh* inquires into the provisions he is carrying on him, and proposes that he might as well call off his laborious journey, pay the sum in his possession to the *shaykh*, and circumambulate him as he might the Ka'ba. For:

> The Ka'ba is the house of His service.
> My form, in which I was created,
> is the house of His secret.
> Since He made the Ka'ba He has never gone into it.
> As to this house: none but the Living has gone into it.
> When you have seen me you have seen God,
> You have circled the Ka'ba of truth.
> To serve me is to praise and obey God:
> think not that God is separate from me.
> Open your eyes and look on me, that you may see
> the light of God in man.[15]

The words first assert an identity, then play up a contrast to the maximum. To begin with, the Ka'ba and the man are identified through the metaphor of the house. The body is a metaphorical home as much as the Ka'ba is literally a house. But this equation spins off into a play of opposites. The Ka'ba, the revered shrine of Islam, stands tenantless. Since the days it was made by God, Rumi provocatively declares, He has not revisited it. The human figure, by contrast, is continually replenished by the grace of Life itself. Stone and Spirit are sketched in sharp mutual contrast.

Sentiments such as these are frowned upon by conservative jurists who detect in them the odour of *shirk*, the attribution of partners to God—in short, idolatry.

However, these debates often turn on a confusion of categories. In a poetics, these notions have a very different status from their counterparts in the propositions of law. In poetry, they assert symbolic truths. Elsewhere, the symbolic function gives way to the claims of literal adherence.

In his study of Ibn al-'Arabi, Henry Corbin has noted that a theology founded on the symbolic imagination is 'equidistant from polytheism' and from 'monolithic, abstract and unilateral monotheism'.[16] The monotheism criticised by Corbin is blind to the plurality of forms implied by symbolic imagination. But there is a further point to be made. A dogmatic interpretation of the sacred is as much an interpretation as anything else. For the object of faith cannot be grasped in itself. It marks the limits, the horizon of human aspiration. It transcends its representation in an image or a concept. But this is precisely what dogmatic religion claims. Ironically, therefore—in Corbin's terms—it 'succumbs to the very idolatry it denounces'.[17]

To a reader who reflects on the full implications of this point, a further question suggests itself. One may ask whether what is said here of religion is not in fact a particular example of human knowledge in general. The battle between a search for truth and dogmatic possession of truth is, after all, ever-present in human history. Are not the issues we have noted here in the specific context of the topic of this essay, a variant, after all, of this more general problem of knowledge?

The more general point will have to wait until the final section of this essay. In the meantime, I would like to elaborate on the point made above of the relationship between critical thought and the symbolic mode. This relationship may be stated in terms of the *existential roots of intellectual or reflective thought.* I wish to demonstrate this relationship, in the classical context, via the work of Sijistani, which provides an excellent, if subtle, example of an intellectual system founded on a symbolism of the sacred.

VI

To say that reason has an existential basis is to recognise a connection between logic or philosophy on the one hand and mythical symbolism on the other. The recognition of myth as myth can only happen from outside rather than within myth. It cannot see itself in these terms any more than the eye can see itself. This recognition belongs to critical thought. But is critical thought at an unbridgeable distance, a magisterial elevation, from what it judges to be mythical? Are we condemned to be heir to two dichotomous discourses, one scientific, the other mythical? Are we left with reason on the one side, and religion on the other? Does not the very fact that rational discourse *recognises* myth as such, suggest, a kinship between them?

We have already considered the thesis above that rational thought is grounded in more primary symbols of existence. Our task here is to show this to be the case with Sijistani. The central feature of Sijistani's thought, like that of other Fatimid thinkers, is its world-picture or cosmology. This is essentially the Neoplatonic scheme adapted to Islamic concepts. In this cosmology, God—the Neoplatonic One—remains wholly transcendent. His first creation is the Intellect, out of which emanates the Soul, which generates Nature.

This world-picture is not peculiar to Sijistani. Similar cosmologies were put forward by philosophers like Farabi, with variations which are of interest only to the specialist. The cosmic principles believed in by authors like Sijistani, Nasir-i Khusraw,

Farabi, and Hamid al-Din Kirmani were thought to be responsible for the movement of heavenly spheres. By personifying these, Muslim philosophers were able to equate them with scriptural concepts, like that of angelic beings. The originality of Ismaili authors lay not in the cosmologies, which they no doubt accepted as objective fact, but in the use they made of them to anchor their religio-political vision in a comprehensive world-picture.

The cosmologies, as we would now have little difficulty in recognising, are mythical. But it is not enough to note the negative aspect of myth. The negative aspect may be seen in the fact that the cosmologies are not objectively scientific. Not only are they not compatible with what we now know of the universe, they are also speculative, with no basis in experimental observation. But this recognition of their mythical as opposed to factual status has a positive dimension. It clears the way to an appreciation of the existential function of myth. This is its spiritual side. Myth expresses the human bond to the sacred. And it expresses it in the only way this can be done: in mythical or poetic metaphors, as opposed to propositions of fact.

To appreciate this dimension of Sijistani's thought, we need to dig beneath his philosophy. Straightforward expositions of his thought do not make this dimension obvious.

Paul Walker's work, for instance, while presenting the salient features of Sijistani's philosophy, is oblivious to the philosophical questions which could be asked *about* the philosophy: about, for instance, the respective place of reason and myth in it, and the relationship between them. In order to bring this hidden issue to the fore, a special effort is needed. This is to play off Sijistani's doctrine against what we might call the *élan* of his thought. For at the heart of Sijistani's thought there is a creative paradox. His philosophical doctrine is monumental; yet this monumental aspect is undercut by its spirit, its *élan*. This creative tension is easily missed unless one attends to it and deliberately plays it up.

What do I mean by saying that the *élan* of Sijistani's thought undercuts the structure of his philosophy? What is meant here is essentially connected to what was said above about the tension between letter and spirit. It is possible for even intellectual systems to become closed and absolute. This happens when they are taken at face-value, i.e., as a body of truths which, once mastered, need no further inquiry, and afford no scope for going beyond them.

Sijistani's thought presents a picture of what the world is like. But the spirit of his thought goes beyond the system that he presents. In the end, therefore, his thought is more than doctrine. Its real significance resides not in the picture of the universe it provides, but in the human quest, the existential or spiritual quest, of which this picture is, as it were, a mythical projection.

This point of view finds support in several elements in his doctrine. The first clue is the doctrine that ultimate reality cannot be known. It is a cardinal tenet of Sijistani's philosophy that God is beyond anything that may be said of Him. This was a tenet common to Neoplatonic thinkers. The Fatimid author, Kirmani, for instance, maintained that God's nature was above all attributes, and these included existence and non-existence. According to Walker, the Intellect, in Sijistani's terms, 'remains ultimately beyond the grasp of all other beings. Thus while great portions of the realm of intellect accede to human, most especially prophetic, penetration, the whole of it will never become accessible.'[18]

In any body of thought, there is an affirmative element, i.e., of what is stated to be the case. But what is stated points, by implication, to what is not thought or known. The boundaries of knowledge have not only an inner but an outer edge. They remind us not only of what they enclose but of what they cannot enclose. As Wittgenstein, nearer our own time, was to maintain: after philosophy has clarified everything, all that is significant remains unclarified. This cannot be stated; it can only be *shown*. The world (i.e., the whole) cannot be the object of knowledge. 'The sense of the world must lie outside the world.'

The last quoted sentence repays careful attention. Wittgenstein speaks of the *sense* of the world, not its *explanation*. Speculative systems explain the world as creation, or in Neoplatonic terms, as a series of emanations. Poetic thought reaches out to 'sense'. It enables 'explanation' to be seen as a representation, on the logical plane, of 'sense', which lies beyond this plane.

Sijistani's philosophy reflects a similar, fundamental reservation about language. Words reflect intellectual realities imperfectly; just as in Plato, physical objects are but poor copies of intellectual essences. Therefore, the text is there to be surpassed. The text is essential, for if it were not there, there would be no going beyond it. But to stop at the text is to disconnect it from its inner life. It is to close off the meaning which lies beyond it and infuses it with life.

There is another creative dimension in Sijistani's thought which is worth noting. As we have seen, his philosophy treats religious ideas as part of a larger whole, deriving from roots which lie deeper. The sovereign place of the Intellect in his thought suggests that these roots are intellectual. But *what*, precisely, are they? They are not spelt out in a way resembling, for instance, the fundamental principles of faith in Sunni and Shi'i creeds. There are, of course, the cosmic principles. These do not form a creed but they amount to a framework for explaining the human condition, and the hope of its redemption through ascent to the Intellect. The fact that this is the ultimate object of his philosophy explains why it can only be alluded to rather than encapsulated in a creed. This is a good reason for suspecting that his real concern is existential. In this scheme of redemption through intellect, there is no substitute for a personal endeavour on the part of each individual. The existential process can be described only in symbolic terms rather than in formal doctrine.

This point leads us to a final, significant polarity in Sijistani's work. To a great extent Sijistani's system, precisely because it is a system, is atemporal. It is synchronic, showing how various parts of the universe fit into one another. Yet the entire system, far from being static, is in fact perpetually on the move. It is stirred and driven by an inner restlessness. The Soul, for instance, is a pale semblance of the Intellect. It thinks sequentially, indeed laboriously, whereas the Intellect intuits essences without having to operate in time. Moreover, the Soul is consumed by a yearning to rise to the superior condition of the Intellect.

This yearning shows its divided nature. On one hand, the Soul is driven by a 'never ending desire for intellect'. Yet it suffers from an eternal incapacity to attain this desire. 'Torn between two conflicting forces, [the] soul is restless and incomplete. It will always require something it does not yet have in order to achieve perfection. It is potentially something but never exactly that something.'[19]

Thus, it looks two ways. It gazes above towards an ideal, and peers below into the darkness and corruption of matter. It is, in fact, already mired in the turgidity of matter. Through this downward, gravitational pull it has turned 'forgetful' of its lofty origin. Now, where do these ideas belong if not to mytho-poetic thinking—this 'forgetfulness' of one's origin, and a lingering 'memory' of it? For we never know our origin scientifically, as we know the origin of the butterfly in a caterpillar. What is in question here is not something external to us, nor a part of us, but we ourselves, the whole of us. This is not a subject suited to the language in which we connect subject to object—where we as subjects speak about what is 'out there', what is other than us. The allusiveness of poetic language is, on the other hand, characteristically suited to expressing the self's sense of its own destiny. It does not describe an object, but evokes an ideal.

Thus the Intellect, towards whom, according to Sijistani, all life strains forward, may itself be seen as a symbol. It is not one object among others, but the focus of an existential striving. It is the focus of *self*-interpretation: the pole star guiding the course of human life.

We encountered these themes earlier in our analysis of the opening passage of the *Mathnawi*. This resemblance is at first sight surprising. Philosophical thought and mysticism were very different traditions in Islam. Often they were mutually hostile. What unites the Neoplatonic philosophy of Sijistani with mystical or devotional poetry is the existential element. Otherwise they are far apart. For philosophy was an urban, intellectual pursuit; whereas mystical and devotional poetry belongs to the world of folk-literature. But the symbolism of 'return' in Sijistani, articulated as it is in learned terms, has resonances in literary forms far removed from his. There is, for instance, the well-known folk-tale which speaks of a lion, long-accustomed to living as a sheep among sheep, who at last gains self-recognition on hearing himself roar, in telling contrast to the bleating of the sheep. (In the jargon of contemporary psychology, he literally finds his voice.) This story is told succinctly in an Indo–Ismaili poem (*ginan*) attributed to Pir Shams:

> The scarlet lion
> forgot his form.
> Amongst sheep,
> a sheep he became.

At first sight, to speak of Sijistani's work and the *ginan* literature in one breath seems quite incongruous. They belong to very different worlds. The difference is not only one of time, place, and traditions of thought and language. They also inhabit totally different social worlds. Yet, in their existential reference, they share a deep structure in common.

This deep structure is that of a narrative. More specifically, it is a mythical narrative of beginnings and ends. The theme of an incomplete existence, aspiring towards an ideal fulfilment, is characteristically suited to the story-form. For where there is aspiration, there is movement. In language, movement translates itself into narrative. A narrative of origin and end visualises life as a passage from one to the other. The end is represented in symbols of the hereafter. The origin is symbolised as an original innocence, as in the Garden of Eden; or an original unity with the divine, nostalgically recalled in mystical literature, as in the following passage of another Indo–Ismaili poem, attributed to Pir Hasan Kabir al-Din:

> Adam, primordial, invisible.
> Free of attributes, in himself
> Formless.
> You, Lord, are our origin.
> It was our forms
> Which grew asunder.

The duality of origin and end—what was and what shall be— resonates with dual aspects of *present* existence. What a story locates, at one end, in a 'once upon a time', and at the other, 'in a time to come', translates, in the here and now, into a disparity between what one 'essentially' is and what one comes to be in the phenomenal world. (In the poem above, this transposition is helped by the fact that the term *asal*, the Gujarati variant of the Arabic and Persian *asl*, signifies both origin and essence.)

The notion of an original existence and the expectation of a future consummation are a representation, in time, of an inner movement of self towards self. The power of mytho-poetic narration lies precisely in this: it speaks at one and the same time, thanks to its symbolic resources, of the cosmic and the existential.

The contrast of this symbolic understanding with orthodox theology should by now be fully apparent. Thus, in speaking of Ibn al-'Arabi's conception of the 'new being', Henry Corbin has rightly remarked: 'this is the other world, or rather, this *already* is the other world. Clearly this is a far cry from the dogmatic religious definition of the 'other world' ... the other world is perpetually engendered *in* this world and *from* this world.'[20]

With these observations, we may now recapitulate the argument in this and the preceding section. Our aim was to inquire into the presuppositions which underlie the significant differences in the intellectual history of Islam—in classical Islamic history. Our bird's eye-view has shown us that from a comparatively early period, there was a tension between a traditionalist culture which demanded submission to a textual tradition, and a rationalism which invited the individual to cultivate his intellectual faculties and so to realise and comprehend the rational order of reality. Our further investigation of some of the chief specimens of rationalism in the classical history of Islam showed how a realisation of this rational order could involve two further ideas. One is that of symbolic interpretation. The other is that of the relation of philosophical reason to the symbolism of the sacred. This second issue led us to explore the underlying bond between reflective thought and existential symbolism. In so doing we saw an extension of the significance of poetics to the domain of reason.

One does not have to agree with this argument in its entirety to appreciate a very general point. A historian of Islam has put it in these words:

Implicit in the agreement that Islam was a religiously sanctified way of life lived in accordance with God's will as set out in scripture was a

profound disagreement about the boundaries between revealed truth
and human interpretation, the requirements of faith and the use of
reason, the degree of man's submission to God or his autonomy in
living a Muslim life. The same outer life ... could imply radically different forms of spirituality.[21]

This general observation, with which this essay is in agreement,
is something we have tried to elucidate by an analysis of the relevant concepts. But is the importance of these concepts confined
to the history of religion? Do they have any role whatsoever in a
more general analysis of culture? In the next section we turn our
attention to this question.

VII

If there is a single word which captures the philosophical outlook
opposed to an open, pluralist, and rational culture—an outlook
also antithetical, therefore, to poetics as described here—that word
is reductionism. This term is more useful to us than a theological
term because it helps us to identify a more general phenomenon,
one common to religious as well as non-religious contexts. This
broader perspective will mean that the theological portion of the
discussion in the foregoing pages will logically be subsumed into
the wider point of view recommended here.

Henry Corbin, who does not engage with issues of modernity,
makes one interesting, critical remark, though isolated, linking
medieval theology and the modern secular world. He suggests
that the 'abstract monotheism [of orthodox theology] and [secu-
lar] monism reveal a common totalitarian trend.'[22] By 'abstract
monotheism' he means the doctrine of creation *ex nihilo* (creation from nothing). Corbin distinguishes this view from Ibn
al-'Arabi's doctrine of spiritual creativity. And he wonders whether
the loss of this dimension 'is not the hallmark of our laicized world
for which the foundations were laid by the preceding religious
world, which precisely was dominated by this characteristic idea
of the Creation.'[23]

We need not adopt Corbin's entire approach to appreciate the
astuteness of this particular observation. In essence, his point is
that a certain kind of theology, and a certain kind of secular

ideology which is heir to this theology, share a fundamental, common trait. This trait is monism, the doctrine of a single truth. And monism has a logical affinity with psychological and political totalitarianism.

I am wholly in agreement with this thesis. However, it needs to be complemented by a further observation. There is more than one trend of thought and sensibility in modern culture. Modernity is not, any more than theology, monolithic. In fact, just as a contrast between tendencies towards monism and pluralism was, as we saw, characteristic of Islamic history, a similar tension has been equally characteristic of the history of modern culture.

One form of reductionism which dominated the intellectual culture of the West in recent times is that of the philosophical school known as Positivism. Positivism has many strands in it, but here we need to note only its general characteristics. Essentially, Positivism was a doctrine which took the methods and outlook of modern, natural science as the model for all knowledge. The ground for this canonisation of physical science had first been prepared by the great German philosopher Immanuel Kant. In noting this Kantian influence, one cannot but be struck by a sense of irony. For it was far from Kant's mind to belittle the ideas which lie at the heart of the Abrahamic faiths—ideas like that of God, soul, and immortality.

Since Kant's position on these issues is both interesting and deeply influential in the intellectual culture of modernity, it is worth attempting to summarise it here. This is a thankless task, for his thought is exceedingly complex. Nonetheless, the following sketch outlines the core of his position on issues related to the present discussion.

The target of Kant's criticism was not faith but theology. More specifically, it was metaphysics, whose influence had thoroughly penetrated medieval philosophy and theology. Metaphysics is a rational, speculative system which proposes a comprehensive theory of reality. Such a system was the one proposed by Plato. Aristotle's philosophy, though giving weight to pragmatism side by side with theory, assigns to metaphysics the highest place in the hierarchy of different forms of knowledge. This classification was duly echoed later by philosophers like Avicenna.

The essence of Kant's assessment of metaphysics is that it reflects an unavoidable urge on the part of the human mind to go beyond experience. This is true, in Kant's view, of concepts like God, soul, or a rationally ordered universe. What they are meant to refer to form the basis of the totality of human experience. This urge of the human mind to understand what it could only understand if it were to transcend itself, shows a dilemma in which it is perennially caught. It is tormented by questions which invite the mind to survey the totality of human experience from outside. However, this is impossible. Kant's statement of this predicament of human reason opens his magisterial treatise, *Critique of Pure Reason*: 'Human reason has this peculiar fate that in one species of its knowledge it is burdened by questions which, as prescribed by the very nature of reason itself, it is not able to ignore, but which, as transcending all powers, it is also not able to answer.'[24]

However, as the mind cannot contemplate what lies beyond the world of experience *except in terms of that experience*, its attempt to reach the ultimate bedrock of reality is doomed to failure. Metaphysical theories are, on this account, an instance, as it were, of short-circuiting. They spell out what cannot be spelled out, for the activity of 'spelling out' is supposed to be one of the results or products of what it is that it seeks to describe.

This point is reinforced by another element in Kant's thought. In discussing concepts such as space, time, and causality, Kant pointed out that we never *perceive* any of these. However, we always perceive objects as being in space, events as occurring in time, and natural occurrences as being linked by cause and effect. The net conclusion to be drawn from this is that we can never know things as they are in themselves. We only know them as they appear to us. This point may become clearer if we think, by analogy, of how differently the world might look to creatures whose visual apparatus is able to pick up light-waves outside the spectrum visible to the human eye; or whose ears can detect frequencies of sound below the threshold of the human ear. In short, the world, which is an appearing (phenomenal) world, is from the very beginning organised in categories of experience. While 'our knowledge must conform to objects,' Kant says, 'it is also true that objects must conform to our knowledge.'

Of what the world is like *in itself*, therefore, we can say nothing. This is why pronouncements on ultimate reality, which are the stock-in-trade of metaphysics or natural theology, are misguided. The light dove, as Kant exquisitely puts it, 'cleaving the air in her free flight and feeling its resistance,' might dream fondly of soaring in empty space. This hope, a form of metaphysical pathos, is moving; but it is in vain.

This does not make the notions of metaphysics altogether illegitimate. The idea of a rationally ordered world, for example, is not a finding of science: no science can take on the 'world' as its object. The world, as a whole, cannot be 'known'. But what is not the object of knowledge reveals its true nature, in a Kantian critique, as an ideal. An ideal, by definition, is not a fact. However, it provides the orientation in the absence of which the pursuit of knowledge of facts might well become impossible. Thus, to complete the example of the concept of the world as a rational whole: although this is not a subject of scientific knowledge, it is essential to it as a governing concept. Unless the world is assumed to be a rational order, scientific research might well become impossible. Devoid of direction or orientation, incentive or vision, it would be drained of its inner momentum.

Kant thought that concepts of faith, like that of God and immortality of the soul, were similar. Only in this case, these concepts were conditions for the possibility not of theoretical, but of practical reason. They are not objects of knowledge, but regulative ideas which make moral life possible. Kant was himself a religious man, although his rejection of scholastic proofs for the existence of God, so beloved of medieval philosophers, might give the opposite impression to a less than careful reader. Kant himself was only too conscious of this. He was at pains to point out that his motive for discrediting these proofs was far from impious. He had only 'found it necessary to deny knowledge so as to make room for faith.'

I have referred to Kant because he marks a watershed between the thought-forms of the classical world—of the Abrahamic faiths as well as Greco–Roman culture—and of the modern world of the Enlightenment. As far as faith is concerned, his thought is anti-dogmatic, rejecting the notion of absolute knowledge, and insisting on an element of the provisional in faith. For the idea of faith contains an idea of mystery. When the sense of mystery is jettisoned, faith gives way to dogma. However, Kant's philosophy also reflects some of the central dilemmas pervading the entire history of the culture of the modern West.

It is significant to note that Kant's view of the intellectual content of faith grants it only a notional status. It denies that the ideas at the heart of religious faith can be anything but regulative of morality. However, whether we take these ideas as literally or symbolically true, it can hardly be denied that whether we subscribe to them or not makes a profound difference not only in how one acts, but how one conceives of the universe, human nature, and the human self. In other words, the difference between. a man of faith and his opposite counterpart is not only in how he believes he should act, and why, but in his understanding of the good life; and beyond that, in his understanding of the place of the good in the scheme of things entire. Kant does not grant this, and this is not unrelated to the absence of a place, in his philosophy of religion, of a poetics of religious experience. It is also fundamentally connected with a widely noted dichotomy in modern culture, between nature and morality. It is one of the central tenets of Kantian philosophy that nature has nothing to do with good and evil. This principle is pursued, in Kant's moral philosophy to the point where nature *within man*, i.e., his passions and inclinations, have no legitimate role in moral life. The only truly relevant factor in moral life is the will to do the call of duty. This is a rational will, uncompromised by passion or emotion.

This Kantian view anticipates a more general characteristic of modernity, namely its strict separation of the realm of facts from the realm of values. We unconsciously show the hold of this dichotomy on our minds when we speak, as we often do and with disapproval, of someone making 'value-judgements'. By this we usually mean that one is being subjective, as we assume that values are not objective, and have nothing to do with facts. (It is only fair to add that Kant never thought of moral standards as subjective: universality was for him a defining feature of the moral will, though we do not need to examine Kant's moral philosophy here.) One place where the influence of this dichotomy may be observed is in the world of learning. I have in mind the dichotomy between science and ethics, or more generally, between scientific and humanistic studies. This separation is not fundamentally solved by the growing awareness, in our times, of the ethical dilemmas posed by modern advances in science. For while this awareness is no doubt justified and enlightened, it does not mark an essential departure from the assumption that knowledge and ethics are inherently separate realities.

Positivism marked the climax of the disengagement of science (or positive knowledge of the world) from all other interpretations of the world. An extreme form of this Positivism was the doctrine known as Logical Positivism.

The basic tenet of Logical Positivism was summed up in the Principle of Verification. What this said was as follows. For a proposition to be meaningful, it must be either true or false. Truth and falsity are decided by empirical verification. This may be done either here and now (as with the statement that water boils at 100°C at sea-level) or in principle, when the tools for verification are not yet available (as with the assertion that there is life elsewhere in the universe). The statements of metaphysics (e.g., 'The Absolute is Spirit'), theology (e.g., 'There is spiritual resurrection after death'), and ethics (e.g., 'It is wrong to steal') are not open to verification, either now or in principle. We do not know what would constitute a proof or disproof of these assertions; therefore they are meaningless. Ethical propositions are, it was admitted, all-important in society, but they say nothing about reality. They only express the feelings of those who subscribe to them. When different people in a culture feel alike, we get shared moral norms. When they differ, no appeal to facts will by itself lead to agreement.

There are a number of critical observations to make about this theory. First, it is obvious that this theory would arise only in an age overwhelmingly impressed by the achievements of physical science. It would be idle to deny these achievements: they are the most spectacular accomplishments of our times. However (and this is the second point), as a picture of science, this is a gross over-simplification. It does not correspond to how science actually works. As Karl Popper, one of the staunchest champions of science in recent times emphasised, 'a science is not merely a 'body of facts'. It is, at the very least, a collection, and as such it is dependent upon the collector's interests, upon a point of view. In science, this point of view is usually determined by a scientific theory; that is to say, we select from the infinite variety of facts, and from the infinite variety of aspects of facts, those facts and those aspects which are interesting because they are connected with some more or less preconceived scientific theory.'[25]

Moreover, it is important to note that the Positivist valuation of science is not itself scientific. It is a philosophical and hence, more generally, a cultural attitude. It is an attitude *towards* science, an image of science. This becomes clear if we consider a question which was often asked by critics of this doctrine: how is the principle of verification to be verified? It is obvious that it cannot be verified. Judged by its own criterion, the principle of verification is clearly not a proposition of knowledge. It reflects a decision as to what is to *count* as knowledge. This decision is not directly supported by science, but by a culture in which a particular view of truth, of what is successful and important in human life and what is not, had come to prevail.

In its refusal to treat religious, ethical, or artistic language as anything to do with facts or knowledge of facts—in a nutshell, with objective reality—Logical Positivism is an excellent example of a reductionism, characteristic of the culture of secular modernity. It testifies to one of the central features of secular modernity. This is its unwillingness, or incapacity, to appreciate interpretations of reality which fall outside a narrowly conceived, physicalistic model. Its treatment of ethics also reflects the incapacity, in much of modern culture, to see the moral life as resting on anything more firm, enduring, or objective than the volition—the choices—of individuals. The picture it calls to mind in this respect is of men and women browsing, as it were, in a supermarket of values, there to pick and choose ethical options on the basis of nothing more substantial than the inclinations of their individual personalities.

I hope I have said enough in these pages to forestall the misconception that this essay takes the side of tradition against modernity, eulogising the 'spirituality' of the former and lamenting the 'materialism' of the latter. This particular bandwagon is not one which I recommend climbing. It is not nostalgia for a mythical past but a drive against reductionism of any kind—whether theological or secular—which inspires the argument of this essay.

We must not mention the reductionist impulses in modern society without taking note, at the same time, of substantial intellectual currents, also at the heart of modern culture, which flow in an opposite direction. The promising aspect of these currents lies in their focus on the subject of language.

Why study language? The royal road, in our times, to a fuller and richer vision of reality is to appreciate the actual variety, the concrete scope of the ways in which human beings have experienced what surrounds them, and what lies within themselves. Language is the house of this experience.

To pay attention to language is a way, then, of reopening the question of what it means to be human. To appreciate the *varieties* of language is to appreciate the diversity of ways in which the question of what it means to be human has been explored in the concrete life of the world's civilisations. It is to begin from 'here' rather than 'there'—not with groundless pronouncements about another world, but with what human beings have said and sung, hoped and feared, dreamt and imagined, in the here and now. The best chance of renewed contact, in our times, with the full scope of being human, lies in taking patient note of the actual testimony of human lives and cultures.

It is idle to imagine that this can be done by wiping the slate clean and starting altogether afresh. Human beings belong to traditions, and traditions are built on presuppositions. One invariably begins at the middle, not at the beginning. Absolute beginnings, however desirable, are practically impossible. Starting from within a tradition, and being sensitive to its full scope and variety, it is possible to ensure its unpredictable creativity—to preserve it, in other words, not as a storehouse of sediments, but as a reservoir of possibilities.

In what is called hermeneutic philosophy, restoring the breadth of language is seen as the major challenge of our times. In a utilitarian culture, the instrumental use of language—words as technical means to technical ends—is liable to overshadow all other functions and possibilities of human speech, and finally to drive them into oblivion. In a world of techniques, it is easy to lose sight of what we might call existentially expressive language. It is in this language that man articulates his experience of his essential being. It is a language which does not seek to control or manipulate being, but to express, simply, its depth and plenitude.

Poetic speech is a testimony to this expressive power of language. It is also a witness to the plenitude of being, celebrated in an abundance of meaning. Paul Ricoeur has put this in a remarkably succinct manner: 'It is the task of poetry to make words mean as much as they can and not as little as they can.'[26] The poetic expression of religious experience—of the mystery of being—is a testimonial to the power of language to say more rather than less, and to evoke continuing reserves of meaning. We have seen how the Islamic context offers rich and ample testimony to this power.

In the simplest terms, to appreciate the variety of language, in the face of the temptation to reductionism—a temptation regularly brought to us by the religious and secular fundamentalisms of our day—is to recover, in the broadest sense, the spiritual dimension of life. The contemporary moment, in Ricoeur's words, is that of forgetfulness:

> ... forgetfulness of the signs of the sacred, loss of man himself insofar as he belongs to the sacred ... It is in the age when our language has become more precise, more univocal, more technical in a word ... it is in this very age ... that we want to recharge our language ... It is not regret for the sunken Atlantides that animates us, but hope for a recreation of language. Beyond the desert of criticism, we wish to be called again.[27]

There is one final point I wish to add on the relationship of poetics to our ongoing history. Poetic expression shows religious experience to be not a state but a search—a search for the truth of being. Like all literature, poetic speech is not just something to be relished, but it is also something to be evaluated. What it says about being must be tested against one's own life-experience, and against our up-to-date knowledge of the world. There is a place here, then, for verification, so long as we understand this notion broadly, and not along a narrow, *a priori* model. The verification which applies here is an existential one. This does not mean 'emotional' as opposed to 'intellectual', but includes the intellect as its central instrument, though an intellect rooted in the fullness of life.

Verification constitutes a search for truth. To say this is to reject the self-enclosure of language which is characteristic of so much that goes on in faculties of humanities in modern universities. Specifically, it is to reject the wall between science, on the one hand, and religion, ethics, and the arts on the other hand— a division which is one of the problematic legacies of modernity. This is why it is necessary, in the context of the present subject, to beware of falling into the trap of the opposition of religion to reason, and poetry to science. The poetics of religious experience is ultimately inseparable from intellectual creativity in general. If, as Karl Popper has argued, science must, if it is to remain true to itself, perpetually challenge and criticise its own conclusions, so also, in their own way, must religious visions of the world. They must remain receptive to the new knowledge of the world and of the human life which all the branches of learning—the arts and the sciences—daily place at our disposal. To say this is to emphasise the concept of continual creation, a concept in which science, poetry, and religion find a common foundation, mirroring, in the process, the very nature of human existence on earth.

Notes

1. L. Wittgenstein, *Tractatus Logico-philosophicus,* trans. D. F. Pears and B. F. McGuinness (London, 1995 rpr.), p. 72.
2. Qur'an, 24:40.

3.   The leading contemporary philosopher who has done more than anyone else to illuminate these themes is Paul Ricoeur. I must here acknowledge the profound influence of his thought on the core substance of this essay. However, I must add—and this is something that Ricoeur himself would wholeheartedly admit—that his philosophy is centrally informed by its Judaeo-Christian context on the one hand, and its European philosophical ancestry on the other. The two issues which arise if we apply his scheme to an analysis of the Islamic context—the illumination it offers, and the adaptations forced into it by this cross-cultural confrontation—are highly interesting, but beyond the scope of the present essay.

4.   Jalal al-Din Rumi, *The Mathnawi-i Ma'nawi*, ed. and trans. R. A. Nicholson (London, 1925), Book I.ii.1–4.

5.   See, on this point, Paul Ricoeur's extensive analysis in *The Symbolism of Evil*, trans. Emerson Buchanan (Boston, 1969) pp. 232–78.

6.   The *Mathnawi*'s chief translator in English, R. A. Nicholson, evidently guided by Victorian scruples, translated the occasional, earthy elements in Rumi's language into Latin, so as to protect the innocence of minors unschooled in that language. As it turns out, since his translation is the only complete one to date, and as hardly anyone in the English-speaking world now reads that language, he has also performed the dubious service of protecting its adult readership from the entertainment of these passages.

7.   Ibn al-'Arabi, *The Tarjuman al-Ashwaq*, ed. and trans., R. A. Nicholson (London, 1911), XI, vs. 12–15.

8.   Rumi, *Mathnawi*, Book 2, ii.1720–61.

9.   Ira M. Lapidus, *A History of Islamic Societies*, (Cambridge, 1988), p.107.

10.   A recently published and accessible monograph on al-Sijistani's life and thought is Paul E. Walker, *Abu Ya'qub al-Sijistani: Intellectual Missionary* (London, 1996).

11.   Walker, *Abu Ya'qub al-Sijistani*, pp. 28–9.

12.   Ibid., p. 28.

13.   See Henry Corbin, *Creative Imagination in the Sufism of Ibn 'Arabi*, trans. Ralph Manheim (Princeton, 1969), p. 200.

14.   Mahmoud Ayoub, verbal communication.

15.   Rumi, *Mathnawi*, (Book 2, xi. 2245–9).

16.   Corbin, *Creative Imagination*, p. 193.

17.   Ibid., p. 204.

18.   Walker, *Abu Ya'qub al-Sijistani*, p. 37.

19.   Ibid. pp. 41–2.

20.   Corbin, *Creative Imagination*, p. 203.

21.   Lapidus, *A History of Islamic Societies*, p. 105.

22.   Corbin, *Creative Imagination*, p. 203.

23.   Ibid., p. 182

24.   Immanuel Kant, *Critique of Pure Reason*, trans Norman Kemp Smith (London, 1929), p. 7.

25.   Karl Popper, *The Open Society and its Enemies* (5th edition, London 1990), vol. 2, p. 259.

26.   Paul Ricoeur, *Ricoeur Reader: Reflection and Imagination*, ed. Marion J. Valdes (Hemel Hempstead, 1991), p. 449.

27.   Ricoeur, *The Symbolism of Evil*, p. 349.